REALMS OF FANTASY

Malcolm Edwards & Robert Holdstock

Doubleday & Company, Inc.
Garden City, New York 1983

First published in the United States of America by
Doubleday & Company, Inc., 245 Park Avenue, New York,
NY 10017.

Design and Art Direction by Steve Henderson.

Library of Congress Cataloging in Publication Data

Edwards, Malcolm.
  Realms of fantasy.

  1. Fantastic fiction, English—Illustrations.
2. Fantastic fiction, American—Illustrations.
3. Imaginary societies—Illustrations.
4. Geographical myths in literature—Illustrations.
I. Holdstock, Robert.   II. Title.
PR830.F3E38   1983   823'.0876'09   83-45020
ISBN 0-385-18888-9

Printed in Spain, by Cayfosa. Barcelona.
Dep. Leg. B-17110 - 1985

CONTENTS

INTRODUCTION

Fantasy is not easy to define. In this respect it differs from its cousin (some would say its offspring), science fiction, which has a fairly · clear genesis and historical development. In general terms fantasy can only satisfactorily be defined negatively: it is fiction which is *not* realistic, fiction which could *not* have taken place in our world as it is in the present, as we know it to have been in the past, or as we might reasonably suppose it to be in the future.

There is also a *publishing genre* called fantasy, which at present is enjoying a tidal wave of popularity. This fantasy is much narrower in scope: it takes place in an invented world, which may or may not have some doorway to our own, where humans coexist with creatures of myth and legend – giants and dragons and trolls and dwarves and elves – and where heroes with magic talismans save the world from the dark forces of evil. As the distinguished critic Nicholas Lowe has noted, "Fantasy is dominated by mavericks, the wholly individual writers whose work has no direct precursors and stands outside all modern literary traditions. The contemporary notion of the fantasy genre is the invention of hack writers trying to validate their work by preposterous comparison with writers of imaginative genius."

In *Realms of Fantasy* we look in detail at the worlds created by some of those individual and imaginative writers. There are a number of different kinds of fantasy represented, and in the course of this Introduction we will discuss them all, but the most common kind – the one which has inspired most works of real stature – is rooted in our most ancient and enduring literature, that of myth and legend and epic.

All imaginative fiction can be said to have developed from myth and legend – from the tradition by which fireside storytelling became invested with the supernatural, with the men of the tribe, or city, fighting not other men, but the gods and demons and monsters which were believed to roam the distant wastes. Epic fantasy goes back, literally, to the beginning of recorded history: to the earliest known writing, set down in cuneiform on clay tablets in Sumeria in the third millennium BC. The best known of these is the *Epic of Gilgamesh*, discovered by Layard in the mid 19th century. Gilgamesh was, it appears, a real King of Assyria, who had his capital at the city of Uruk; but he is to the early Bronze Age what Arthur is to the later Iron Age - an historical figure invested by legend with supernatural powers. The Gilgamesh of the epic was a giant figure, two parts god and one part man. The god in him makes him wise and powerful, but the part of him that is man makes him mortal. Herein lies the great tragedy: the *Epic of Gilgamesh* is the tale of a man-god who seeks immortality; the tale of the god in the man being betrayed by the weakness and corruption of the man in the god. Gilgamesh roams a landscape where gods and monsters walk abroad, where there are treacherous maidens and powerful wizards. In the process he encounters the Flood, the Ark, and has other fictive experiences which we recognise from early Old Testament writings.

Later, the cultures of ancient Greece also adapted earlier legends. The *Iliad* and the *Odyssey* are classics, of course, and the latter is an inspiring work of fantasy, documenting Odysseus's long and marvellous journey home from the Trojan Wars. The cyclops, dragons, witches, sirens, mysterious islands - all the supernatural ingredients one could wish. Later still, the Arabian tales known collectively as the *One Thousand Nights and A Night* featured a hero who remains popular: Sinbad the Sailor - Sinbad the Tailor. Sinbad's journeys derive strongly from the *Odyssey*, but adapted to the Arabic culture in which they were told. Sinbad is a simple tailor who adventures perilously, against monsters (most famously the giant bird, the roc), gods and men of magic.

One could elaborate the tradition endlessly. Each ancient culture had its body of fantastic myths and legends - the Roman *Aeneid*, the Finnish *Kalevala*, the Persian *Shah Namah*, the Welsh *Mabinogion*, the Teutonic *Nibel-ungenlied*, the Anglo-Saxon *Beowulf* and so forth. In the Middle Ages works such as Malory's *Morte d'Arthur* and Spenser's *Faerie Queene* and Ariosto's *Orlando Furioso* enter the literature, not as legends and myths to be believed, but as individual works of the imagination.

The subsequent literary history of fantasy can only be touched on briefly in this book. Suffice it to say that a number of individual writers and books, such as William Beckford and his novel *Vathek*, provide a thin thread of continuity between the early works mentioned above and modern fantasy, which can be said to have arisen with the romances of William Morris, the pre-Raphaelite poet and writer, advocate of craftsmanship and elaborate design, who is probably most widely known today for his wallpaper patterns. Late in his life he wrote a series of novels set in imaginary medieval worlds - *The Well at the World's End*, *The Wood Beyond the World*, and *The Water of the Wondrous Isle*. After Morris comes the twentieth century and two more maverick writers of great influence: Lord Dunsany and E. R. Eddison. Beginning in 1905 with *The Gods of Pegana* - an odd volume of sketches describing a bizarre, imaginary pantheon of deities - Dunsany published several books of colourful and highly imaginative short stories. In 1922 Eddison published *The Worm Ouroboros,* an immense and rich fantasy novel chronicling the war between the opposed forces of Witchland and Demonland.

These writers established the tradition of epic fantasy in which most of the authors discussed in this book work. There are other traditions too, which we will discuss later, most notably the "lost world" story and the planetary romance. But the traditions mingle, and all the books achieve a similar kind of effect in creating a world apart from our own.

In 1938 Tolkien delivered an important lecture (later published in a revised and enlarged version) called "On Fairy Stories". What he meant by the term "fairy story" was not the kind of nursery tale which the words immediately conjure for us. In his terms the book he was just setting out to write, *The Lord of the Rings*, was a fairy story of epic dimensions; and the lecture can be seen as an advance defence of the value of the enterprise. Tolkien points out that fairy stories do not, on the whole, feature fairies in their cast lists (just as science fiction does not necessarily incorporate scientists or science; in this respect both names are unfortunate). "Most good fairy stories", he says "are about the *adventures* of men in the Perilous Realm." He points out that the identification of fairy stories as children's stories is an unfortunate accident of history, which had (in 1938) a malign effect on the writing of such fiction. Only a maverick would attempt to write such a book for adults.

The achievement of the successful writer of fairy stories, Tolkien says, is that "He makes a Secondary World which your mind can enter. Inside, what he relates is 'true': it accords with the laws of that world."

Fairy stories or not, the works discussed in *Realms of Fantasy* do just this. They build Secondary Worlds, as real and distinct while you are reading as any other fictional world. The writer must not cheat: the laws governing the invented world may be different from those in our own, but they must be applied consistently. If the author simply draws a series of fantastic rabbits out of hats when the hero gets into a tight corner, the work will have no value. Nor will it be any good unless the author builds the Secondary World with enough realism and conviction that while you are reading you can forget that it *is* invented. It is no easy task. Tolkien, of course, succeeded totally, to the point where, when his work became a cult in the late 1960s, aspects of the hippy movement can be seen retrospectively as an attempt to turn the Western world into the cosier and more friendly society of the hobbits (though the pipeweed that was an important part of the process was probably not the same one that Tolkien had in mind).

One way of achieving a distance between the imaginary world and our own is by the use of a different kind of writing style. If, for example, you wish – as William Morris did – to conjure a kind of Medieval Eden, it is natural to give your characters medieval speech patterns, and once you have decided to do that it is difficult to maintain the illusion if you encase the archaic speech in ordinary modern prose. A a result you find yourself writing a kind of ersatz medievalism – odd enough to feel ancient, but modern enough to be comprehensible.

Morris, Dunsany and Eddison all had different styles, but the one thing they had in common was that their writing was elaborate, ornamented, colourful and somewhat archaic. There is not much small talk between their characters: the formal tone does not admit idle chitchat.

Modern fantasy includes a number of styles, but the best works are usually distanced in some comparable (though usually less elaborate) manner. Tolkien writes a fairly clear prose, with few strange words or archaisms, but the rhythms of his writing recall the epics. Peake invokes the claustrophobia of Gormenghast in a dense and extremely visual manner. Wolfe establishes the strangeness and distance of his far future world with a plethora of odd nouns, some of which can be understood or worked out, some of which remain forever alien. Bradbury conjures the fragility of his dying Mars with a delicate, poetic touch. And so on.

Where lesser fantasy writers fall down is that without a gift for language this kind of effect is impossible to attain. Nothing betrays a writer more quickly and completely than a tin ear. What such writers usually emerge with is something along the lines of, "Then went he unto the courtyard, where saw he she to whom he was betrothed." This is the idea that you get the fantasy "tone" if construct you backwards your sentences, while throwing in a few "untos" and "whoms" and "thences" for seasoning. What you actually end up with is a fair approximation of the way people talk in bad Hollywood costume melodramas.

On the other hand, while a distanced style is often favoured by fantasy writers it is not necessary. There is nothing archaic, for instance, about the writing of Robert E. Howard; but then Howard comes from a tradition very different from that which produced, among others, Tolkien. His is the tradition of American pulp magazine action writing.

In many ways Tolkien and Howard can be seen as the two archetypal writers of modern epic fantasy. Tolkien is entirely the product of a classical tradition. As a scholar he was steeped in Old English literature and the myths and legends of Northern Europe. He created his own mythology and body of legend for Middle Earth, and in due course wrote what he would have called an epic fairy story set against that background.

Howard, on the other hand, had limited formal education though he was intelligent and widely read. He wrote fast, and for money. He invented his background as he went along (with the result that it is sometimes inconsistent). He had little thought that the stories would be remembered once the magazines in which they appeared were no longer on sale. His Hyborian Age is a mishmash of different historical epochs and traditions. His gifts were a colourful imagination and a fast, clean writing style.

To call Howard's work epic fantasy seems too high-flown. The other term, coined by Fritz Leiber, seems more appropriate: sword and sorcery. The emphasis is on the adventure. Burroughs, too, was an adventure writer. So· were writers who came after Howard and were influenced by him, such as Leiber and Sprague de Camp, and the many other authors who have written Howard pastiches. Michael Moorcock began his career heavily under the influence of Howard and Burroughs, but his work grew more ambitious as he matured.

Yet for all the differences there are also similarities, and fantasy as it exists today has the ancestral blood of both Tolkien and Howard in its veins (and Tolkien, incidentally, is reported to have read and enjoyed Howard's Conan stories – though Howard, who died before *The Hobbit* was published, had no chance to reciprocate). Writers such as Ursula Le Guin and Gene Wolfe are impeccably serious about their work, yet both have published and read widely within the sf and fantasy genres. They in turn will influence other writers.

Though the works represented in this book are very varied, their settings can be divided into five broad categories, which are worth looking at in a little detail. These are:

Stories set in the ancient past
Stories set in present-day lost worlds
Stories set on other planets
Stories set in the distant future
Stories set in fantasy Earths quite separate from our own but with affinities to it

Stories set in the distant past The idea of lost ancient civilisations remains attractive, even though the increasingly complete archaeological and paleological records does little to support such an idea. Still, we know that Homo sapiens has been around for a good deal longer than the span of recorded history. Surely, in that period, a civilisation might have bloomed somewhere, prospered for a while, and then fallen so completely that no trace has ever been discovered?

The Atlantis legend is attractive because it provides a ready explanation for the absence of evidence: a geological upheaval that swallowed up this primeval civilisation. One might think it exceptionally ill luck for such a civilisation to place itself so squarely and completely in a geological disaster area – but there is a precedent in Minoan Crete, wiped out by the volcanic explosion of Santorini. Other lost worlds of the past – Lemuria, Mu, Gondwanaland – have been chronicled in fiction, and have had people willing to claim their existence as fact. (At present such theories are eclipsed in popularity by the von Daniken school of thought, which claims archaeological puzzles and anomalies as evidence of alien space-travellers visiting our ancient ancestors.)

Robert E. Howard's world of Hyborea and Michael Moorcock's Melniboné are other examples of worlds situated in the forgotten past. Moorcock's civilisation is entirely fabricated; there are no important links between his world and ours (except when he tries to tie his prehistoric and far-future fantasies together through the device of the Eternal Champion). Howard's, by contrast, is picked up piecemeal from different cultures and different periods, the idea being that at some point everything fell apart, and the ancient civilisations we know are the results of slowly putting the pieces back together again.

Stories set in present-day lost worlds. The notion of an enclave of some vanished civilisation surviving in a remote valley somewhere became popular as the map of the world was gradually filled in by explorers. By the end of the 19th century there was not much left: the dense jungles of South America, a few remote regions of Africa, the more inaccessible parts of the Himalayas, little-known and far-away portions of the Asian hinterland. Around the turn of the century – and up until around 1930 – the so-called "lost race" story was immensely popular. Its undisputed master was H. Rider Haggard, who made his name with explorations of African lost worlds – in *King Solomon's Mines, Allan Quartermain* and *She* – and declined in popularity later in his career as he repeated the formula in numerous later books. Haggard established a formula – a discovered manuscript, a series of half-forgotten legends, a slow and arduous journey, and finally the entry into a world where time has stood still. There are to be found beautiful priestesses, evil cults, riches, extinct creatures – and, above all, exciting adventures.

Many other writers followed suit; Conan Doyle and Hilton are among the most original and best-remembered, but most of the popular adventure writers of the early part of the century have at least one such book to their credit. More recently the form has fallen largely into disuse, primarily because it is now nearly impossible to believe in lands beyond the map (what civilisation, however remote, could escape detection by satellite photography?). But the occasional successful variant does still occur. Two recent examples are Richard Cowper's "The Web of the Magi" and Garry Kilworth's "Blind Windows". Cowper goes back in time to write a full-blooded Haggard pastiche; Kilworth adopts a contemporary setting, but uses a remote and inaccessible system of caverns. Even the recent remake of *King Kong* – one of the most popular lost world stories – managed, despite other deficiencies, to come up with an ingenious and convincing rationale for discovering, in the 1970s, a previously overlooked tropical island.

Stories set on other planets. As the terrestrial map was filled in, the alternative to setting up lost worlds was to look outwards and find new worlds, on other planets. Because at the end of the 19th century it seemed likely that Earthlike conditions might be found on Mars (though the world appeared more ancient than Earth), it was to Mars that Edgar Rice Burroughs and his successors exported their adventure tales. The advantage of an other-worldly setting was that you could invent anything you wished; you were not tied down by earthbound possibility. Eddison's *The Worm Ouroboros* is nominally set on Mercury, but this is a device which the author (and reader) soon forgets.

Mars is the fantasy realm discussed in this book, but it can also be argued that much of what is published as science fiction – particularly in recent years – is essentially fantasy which has been exported to the stars. As the *Encyclopedia of Science Fiction* puts it, "Fans of, say, Frank Herbert are not identical with those of J. R. R. Tolkien, but it is safe to guess that the number of readers who have read and enjoyed both authors is a high proportion of their total readership. Although the world of *The Lord of the Rings* allows magic, where that of Herbert's *Dune* does not, the two have in common the creation of an immensely detailed, richly imagined alternate world, in which individual heroism can play an important role... Generic distinctions serve only to obscure the very real likenesses to be found between works of this kind."

Not all sf, by any means, goes in for the kind of Secondary World building characteristic of fantasy, but much of the sf which is most popular certainly does. Books such as Anne McCaffrey's *Dragonflight* and sequels (where dragons are introduced on a distant planet, and given a kind of scientific rationale) or Marion Zimmer Bradley's "Darkover" series or Robert Silverberg's *Lord Valentine's Castle* owe as much to fantasy as they do to the Wells/Verne tradition of sf.

Stories set in the distant future. As we see in Chapter 10, it is possible to achieve the *feeling* of fantasy by going so far into the future that our world is lost in the mists of antiquity. Not all works set in that distant time can be talked of as fantasy – some, such as Olaf Stapledon's *Last and First Men*, which takes us from the present day millions of years into the future, are unarguably sf. In others, however, such as Jack Vance's "Dying Earth" stories, or Michael Moorcock's "Runestaff" books (set in England and France some time after the holocaust) magic can be worked; the old scientific laws no longer hold, or have been superseded. In Gene Wolfe's story of Urth there is advanced science (or remnants of it), but it might as well be magic for all we understand of its workings. The aspect which crucially differentiates these books from far-future sf, though, is the style. They adopt the fantasy technique of formal, distancing language, while sf stories are told in more straight-forward prose whose aim is to familiarise the strange ideas.

Stories set in fantasy Earths. These kinds of fantasies are perhaps the most characteristic. The worlds in which they are set do not pretend any straightforward relationship with our world and the cosmos in which it is set. You could not find them on any map we could draw, either now or in the past or in the future. They inhabit a different realm: the realm of Faerie. Here men live, but they share their lives with those things that in our world are the stuff of myth and legend. Tolkien and Donaldson and Peake and Le Guin write of such worlds (though Peake's is different in that it lacks any supernatural element).

Sometimes it is possible to travel there from here. Thomas Covenant in Stephen Donaldson's books comes from our world and travels to the Land while his terrestrial body lies unconscious. Time passes much more quickly there, so that he can have months of adventures and return to find that only minutes have passed in this world. Lord Dunsany's stories were set in lands not to be found on any map, but the unwary might sometimes wander there; they are "at the edge of the world" or "beyond the fields we know".

Wherever the realms of fantasy are to be found, whether in the purely non-existent landscape of Tolkien and the like, or in the other types of setting we have identified, a similar kind of story can be unfolded. Is that kind of story of value? Or is it merely escapist wish-fulfilment?

Fantasy novels can be enjoyed as works of pure imagination, without any ulterior motive or inner meaning. On that level they are, indeed, pure escapism. In some quarters escapism has become a dirty word, an insult to be levelled at a work of fiction; the disciples of the influential English critic F. R. Leavis have no time for escapism. But there is nothing to deride in it, if it is done well. Reading a good escapist novel is like playing an absorbing game: pure pleasure, enjoyed for its own sake. (It is no accident that some of the newest and most popular board and video games are based on the player's exploration of highly detailed fantasy worlds.) The problem with too much that is today published under the fantasy label is that it is like a shoddy game. If a game has no depth, no scope, no involvement or demands on the player's imagination, it quickly becomes tiresome; so with fantasy.

But good fantasy is not *just* escapism. The qualities which make a Secondary World an attractive and involving place to visit are also qualities which – whether we are conscious of it or not – work on our imaginations at a deeper level. As Ursula Le Guin put it, in an excellent essay on fantasy called "From Elfland to Poughkeepsie": "Its affinity is not with day-dream, but with dream. It is a different approach to reality, an alternative technique for apprehending and coping with existence... It employs archetypes, which, as Jung warned us, are dangerous things ... Fantasy is nearer to poetry, to mysticism, and to insanity than naturalistic fiction is. It is a real wilderness, and those who go there should not feel too safe. And their guides, the writers of fantasy, should take their responsibility seriously."

Malcolm Edwards & Robert Holdstock

ACKNOWLEDGEMENTS

This book would not have been possible without the imaginative efforts of the authors whose creations are featured in its pages. Our thanks and respect to all of them. If you have read the books from which these realms are derived we hope you will enjoy the interpretation given here. If you have not read the books, we hope you will do so at the earliest opportunity. They are as follows:

Middle Earth
The Fellowship of the Ring (1954)
The Two Towers (1954)
The Return of the King (1955)
The Hobbit (1937)
The Silmarillion (1977) by
J. R. R. Tolkien

Lost Worlds
The Lost World by Sir Arthur Conan Doyle (1912)
Lost Horizon by James Hilton (1933)

Gormenghast
Titus Groan (1946)
Gormenghast (1950)
Titus Alone (1959, revised 1970) by
Mervyn Peake

Also of interest: The Inner Landscape (1969), 3 novellas by Brian Aldiss, J. G. Ballard and Mervyn Peake, containing the Titus story "Boy in Darkness", and the Mervyn Peake Society's publication "The Mervyn Peake Review".

Mars
The Sword of Rhianon by Leigh Brackett (1953)
The Martian Chronicles by Ray Bradbury (1950 - also known as The Silver Locusts)
A Princess of Mars (1917)
The Gods of Mars (1918)
The Warlord of Mars (1919)
Thuvia, Maid of Mars (1920) by Edgar Rice Burroughs
Out of the Silent Planet by C. S. Lewis (1938)

Hyborea
Red Nails (1936)
The Hour of the Dragon (1935)
People of the Black Circle (1934) by Robert E. Howard

Atlantis
The Lost Continent by C. J. Cutliffe Hyne (1900)
The Silmarillion by J. R. R. Tolkien (1977)
The Serpent (1963)
Atlan (1965)
The City (1966) by Jane Gaskell

Melniboné and Elric's Multiverse
The Stealer of Souls (1963)
Stormbringer (1965)
Elric of Melniboné (1972)
The Sailor on the Seas of Fate (1976)

The Knight of Swords (Corum) (1971)
The Queen of Swords (1971)
The King of Swords (1971)

The Jewel in the Skull (Hawkmoon) (1967)
The Mad God's Amulet (1968)
The Sword of the Dawn (1968)
The Runestaff (1969)

The Eternal Champion (Erekosë) (1970)
Pheonix in Obsidian (1970) by Michael Moorcock (a selection only, comprising the initial volumes of Corum and Hawkmoon)

Earthsea
A Wizard of Earthsea (1968)
The Tombs of Atuan (1971)
The Farthest Shore (1973)

The Wind's Twelve Quarters (1975)
The Language of the Night (1979-non fiction essays) by Ursula Le Guin

The Land
Lord Foul's Bane (1977)
The Illearth War (1977)
The Power That Preserves (1977)

The Wounded Land (1981)
The One Tree (1982)
White Gold Wielder (1983) by Stephen Donaldson

Urth
The Shadow of the Torturer (1980)
The Claw of the Conciliator (1981)
The Sword of the Lictor (1981)
The Citadel of The Autarch (1983)

The Fifth Head of Cerberus (1972)
The Castle of the Otter (1983 - non fiction)

The Night Land by William Hope Hodgson (1912)
The Dying Earth by Jack Vance (1950)
The Eyes of the Overworld by Jack Vance (1966)

Chapter One

MIDDLE EARTH

Illustrated by
Paul Monteagle

"But everywhere he looked he saw the signs of war. The Misty Mountains were crawling like anthills: orcs were issuing out of a thousand holes. Under the boughs of Mirkwood there was deadly strife of Elves and Men and fell beasts. The land of The Beornings was aflame; a cloud was over Moria; Smoke rose on the borders of Lórien.

"All the power of the Dark Lord was in motion ... turning south again he beheld Minas Tirith. Far away it seemed, and beautiful: white-walled, many-towered, proud and fair upon its mountain seat; its battlements glittered with steel, and its turrets were bright with many banners. Hope leaped in his heart. But against Minas Tirith was set another fortress, greater and more strong. Thither, eastward, unwilling his eye was drawn. It passed the ruined bridges of Osgiliath, the grinning gates of Minas Morgul, and the haunted Mountains, and it looked upon Gorgoroth, the valley of terror in the Land of Mordor. Darkness lay there under the Sun. Fire glowed amid the smoke. Mount Doom was burning, and a great reek rising. Then at last his gaze was held: wall upon wall, battlement upon battlement, black, immeasurably strong, mountain of iron, gate of steel, tower of adamant, he saw it: Barad-Dûr, Fortress of Sauron."

J. R. R. Tolkien
THE FELLOWSHIP OF THE RING

The story of *The Lord of the Rings* – that is, its development as a publishing phenomenon, not the work itself – is without parallel in modern literature. A long novel of a then unfashionable kind, published in a small edition without expectation of commercial success, it gradually built a following, developed slowly into a cult, exploded into bestsellerdom well over a decade after its appearance, then proceeded to become the centre of a Tolkien industry worth many millions, which even now, nearly 30 years after the publication of *The Fellowship of the Ring* (1954), shows few signs of recession. When *The Silmarillion* finally appeared in 1977 it was, perhaps, the most eagerly awaited book of the decade, and its first printing of half-a-million copies in hardcover in the English language was unprecedented. Tolkien, of course, did not live to see the appearance of the book which, more than any other, can be said to have been his life's work, having been begun as early as 1917: the manuscripts were edited for publication by his son Christopher Tolkien. But there is certainly irony in the fact that this book, the biggest hardcover bestseller ever, was, in an earlier form, rejected some 40 years earlier by the same publishers, Allen & Unwin, who eventually produced it in the UK. They said it was unpublishable. A double irony is that in a sense they were right, for *The Silmarillion* is also without doubt the least read of Tolkien's major works.

The essential facts of Tolkien's life are simply told. John Ronald Reuel Tolkien was born in South Africa in 1892. His family moved to England when he was young, and he was educated at King Edward VI School Birmingham and Exeter College Oxford, gaining his BA in 1915 and his MA in 1919. He proceeded to an academic career of some distinction, being a Professor of Anglo Saxon at Oxford University from 1925 to 1945, and becoming Merton Professor of English Language and Literature at the same university until his retirement in

Preceding pages: *The Mines of Moria, or Khazad-dûm, once the great city of the dwarves. They sought* mithril – *true-silver – but delved too deep and brought about their doom.*

Opposite: *Rivendell, the home of the Elf-lord Elrond, "the Last Homely House East of the Sea". Set between the River Loudwater and the Misty Mountains, surrounded by trees and flowers, it is "a perfect house...", a cure for weariness, fear and sadness.*

1959. He died in 1973. As an academic his contributions were significant, if not precisely major: the most notable were the critical text of *Sir Gawain and the Green Knight* which he edited with E. V. Gordon, and his paper "Beowulf: the Monster and the Critics". In the English faculty at Oxford he was known as a conservative, even reactionary force, resisting moves to modernize the syllabus – "modern" in this context indicting anything much after Shakespeare! This would not be of much interest except that the same kind of conservatism, as we shall see, is one of the driving forces of *The Lord of the Rings*.

In 1937 Tolkien published his children's novel *The Hobbit*, in which he drew on the background he had been developing on and off during the previous twenty years. It was a lasting success, and indeed if his subsequent books had never appeared he would still be remembered as the author of a modern children's classic. It is a colourful fantasy, full of dwarves and wizards and goblins and elves and dragons, telling of a quest undertaken to restore the dwarves to their mountain kingdom and treasure from which the dragon Smaug has driven them. The most unusual feature is the race of hobbits, which unlike the other elements are Tolkien's own invention. Only half the height of humans, inclined to rotundity, good-natured, given to eating, pipe-smoking and jollity, they are ideal subjects for a children's novel. They are of the same order of height as children, for one thing, so that the events of the story are viewed from a child's perspective, to whom Men are tall and somewhat forbidding. And hobbits are child-like, simple in their needs and their psychology. Bilbo Baggins, the hobbit at the centre of the story, is an unlikely figure for a hero – a respectable, stay-at-home sort of figure – and that, too, provides a vital element of identification.

In terms of what is to follow in *The Lord of the Rings*, the most significant event in *The Hobbit* is Bilbo's encounter with the evil but pitiable Gollum by an underground lake. Only in the subsequent books do we discover that Gollum was once a hobbit himself; here, he is a trickster – perhaps more nasty than truly evil – who intends to kill Bilbo and take his Elvish sword. Instead it is Bilbo who tricks Gollum and steals his magic ring, which makes the wearer invisible. The ring is very helpful in the subsequent adventures, but it is only in *The Lord of the Rings* that it comes into its own, when its destruction is necessary if the forces of evil are not to overrun the world.

The transition from *The Hobbit* to *The Lord of the Rings* is not altogether easy to make. Events which in the first book seemed comparatively straightforward are revealed to be part of a story of epic grandeur and scope. A simple talisman – the ring – becomes a symbol of the corrupting nature of power, and Gollum (its long-time possessor) an awful warning of the kind of creature one who permits himself to become corrupted may turn into. Gandalf the wizard, instead of being an eccentric (and occasionally somewhat dotty) figure, becomes instead the rallying point for the forces of good against evil.

In comparing the two works it is possible to gain insights into how a fantasy can be on the one hand enjoyable but quite simple, and on the other can be developed into a whole world into which readers can immerse themselves. One of the unfortunate things about Tolkien's many imitators is that they aim for the grand scale of *The Lord of the Rings*, but only achieve the level of complexity of *The Hobbit*. Tolkien knew better than they the difference between a book for children and one for adults.

If one has read *The Hobbit*, though, it is necessary to make certain allowances in reading *The Lord of the Rings*. Most importantly, it is hard to believe that Gandalf, recognising the power and significance of Bilbo's ring, leaves it with him for some 60 years (the time which elapses between the end of one book and the beginning of the other) until its destruction is both crucial and extremely difficult to accomplish. Tolkien slides

around this, but one is forced to conclude that Gandalf should have acted before he did. Or perhaps it is fairer to recognise that even the most elaborate acts of sub-creation (the term used by Tolkien to describe the invention of a whole Secondary World like his Middle Earth) may fail to be completely self-consistent when they must also be used as a background for a piece of story-telling.

The opening scenes of *The Lord of the Rings* are deceptively homely and bucolic. It begins in the Shire, an isolated and rural part of Middle Earth where the hobbits live out lives untouched by much knowledge of (or even curiosity about) the great outside world. Gandalf the wizard is known to them as an occasional visitor, but to them he is just an old man with a talent for making fireworks. The distant world of Men and Elves, Dwarves and Orcs, is as remote to them as darkest Africa or far Cathay would have been to English village-folk in Elizabethan times.

But the One Ring is in the Shire, and Sauron is searching for it. "He has at last heard, I think, of *hobbits* and the *Shire*," says Gandalf. "The Shire – he may be seeking for it now, if he has not already found out where it lies."

So hobbits must venture out into the great outside world, which is revealed as the story progresses in more and more grandeur. Its geography – which has set a trend for later fantasies – is simple and immense. Much of it is mysterious and seemingly uninhabited. The further wastes to the East and South are realms of men of whom we see little; on Tolkien's maps they appear featureless. But

Opposite: *"They stood upon a heap of stones, gazing at the dark rock of Orthanc, and its many windows, a menace still in the desolation that lay all about it. The waters had now nearly all subsided. Here and there gloomy pools remained covered with scum and wreckage; but most of the wide circle was bare again, a wilderness of slime and tumbled rock, pitted with blackened holes, and dotted with posts and pillars leaning drunkenly this way and that."* Isengard itself is carved, bowl-like, from the side of a hill.

the lands between the Shire and Mordor are richly and variously inhabited.

The nearly impassable line of the Misty Mountains runs for hundreds of miles from north to south, dividing the comparatively tranquil western lands (where the Shire is) from the more turbulent east. Far to the south there is a gap in the range; otherwise they can only be crossed by a difficult mountain pass or by the underground passage through the Mines of Moria. Beyond lies the great river Anduin, the Nile of Middle Earth, which has immense falls.

The various realms are sharply divided by geography as well as populace. Lorien is the home of the Elves, a wood of tall and graceful mallorn trees, among whose branches the Elves build their dwellings. Rohan is a great grassy plain, ruled over by men who virtually live on horseback. To the south, separated by the Anduin, are the kingdoms of Gondor and Mordor. Gondor is the great realm of Men, its cities wonders of white towers and colourful banners. Mordor, to the east, is enclosed by mountains, black, volcanic, evil. It is only

necessary to glance at a map of Middle Earth to see that no good will come out of Mordor.

It is hardly necessary to describe in any detail the story of *The Lord of the Rings*. The Dark Lord, Sauron, has risen in his Eastern kingdom of Mordor. The ring, if he gets his hands on it, will give him a power which will be irresistible. It must be destroyed. The only place where it can be destroyed is in the heart of Sauron's domain. Therefore a company of hobbits and elves and dwarves and men (and Gandalf) is formed to carry out the deed. On the way they must pass through an increasingly dangerous world, which all around them is falling into conflict and disarray. The course of events leaves the responsibility for destroying the ring in the hands of two of the hobbits - on the face of it the people least suited, by temperament and training, for such a task. But they accomplish it, though at the end it is a piece of luck which effects its destruction, and with it the fall of Sauron.

It is fruitless to deny the power of Tolkien's vision or the effect it has had on a growing number of readers. The central, crucial fact

Above: *Long ago there was a great battle between Elves and Men and Orcs. Later the Marshes expanded, swallowing up the graves. Now, beneath the stagnant surface of the water, the dead lie – grim faces and evil, noble faces and sad, all rotting, all dead.*

about the story is that the world in which it takes place feels *real*. It has elements of Anglo-Saxon, Norse and Teutonic myth, and elements from Tolkien's imagination, but these tend to give the story and its background solidity. It is not our world, but it derives from some of the same well-springs as our world. Most importantly, it is a world in which Tolkien had immersed himself for most of his adult life, so that it is reasonable to infer that for him its fictive reality was in its way as great as the reality of the outside world. He went beyond the point where he was making up his world, to the point where he was the chronicler of its history. The moral threat posed by Sauron and his forces therefore seems quite as real as that posed by, say, Hitler (though to draw parallels between the two, as some critics

have tried to do, is to misrepresent Tolkien; allegory did not interest him in the least).

It would be untrue to say, however, that Tolkien has received unanimous praise. Perhaps the first major dissenter was American critic Edmund Wilson, who in 1956 wrote an article entitled, "Ooh, Those Awful Orcs". Later, in a book about epic fantasy, Lin Carter quotes American writer Fritz Leiber: "There's no arguing that a vast number of people ... are tremendously and enduringly enthusiastic about Tolkien's trilogy, yet I do meet quite a few whose reactions are much like my own. We almost always start with, 'The ents are great! Oh boy, yes. And that first part of the quest with the black riders in the distance and Strider a mystery – that's great too. Oh, and yes, the first appearance of the Nazgul and the Balrog ...' At about which point the silence begins and we search our memories and look at each other rather guiltily – exciting things *should* spring to mind, but they don't ..."

A stronger criticism of Tolkien and his work is voiced by one of the authors whose own books are discussed elsewhere in this volume,

Michael Moorcock. In an essay on fantasy entitled "Epic Pooh" he pulls few punches: "He sees the petit bourgeoisie, the honest artisans and peasants, as the bulwark against Chaos. These people are always sentimentalised in such fiction because, traditionally, they are always the last to complain about any deficiencies in the social status quo …

"…It is moderation which ruins Tolkien's fantasy and causes it to fail as a geniune romance. The little hills and woods of that Surrey of the mind, the Shire, are 'safe', but the wild landscapes everywhere beyond the Shire are 'dangerous'. Experience of Life itself is dangerous. *The Lord of the Rings* is a pernicious confirmation of the values of a morally bankrupt middle-class … *The Lord of the Rings* is much more deep-rooted in its infantilism than a good many of the more obviously juvenile books it influenced. It is Winnie-the-Pooh posing as an epic … This is not to deny that we find courageous characters in *The Lord of the Rings*, or a willingness to fight Evil – but somehow those courageous characters take on the aspect of retired colonels at last drawn to write a letter to *The Times* – and we are not sure – because Tolkien cannot really bring himself to get close enough to his proles and their satanic leaders – if Sauron and Co. are quite as evil as we're told. After all, anyone who hates hobbits can't be all bad."

Together these add up to a fairly total criticism of Tolkien's work: it is morally bankrupt, small-minded, conservative and not even very memorable. It is hard to imagine why *anyone* would want to read it, let alone the millions who have done! Yet it must be said that there is some substance to the criticisms.

On first reading, particularly if he is encountered in adolescence, the scale and sweep and conviction of Tolkien's story carry the reader through its 1,000 plus pages triumphantly. One may reread with equal enjoyment, lingering over favourite scenes. Yet even devoted Tolkien fans find that on subsequent readings the spell begins to fade. There are scenes in *The Fellowship of the Ring* which are undoubtedly a triumph, and few would argue that the journey through the underground Mines of Moria – and Gandalf's

apparent death in combat with the Balrog – is the most powerful episode in the whole story. Following on the effective first encounters with the Black Riders and the barrow-wight, Tolkien has succeeded in establishing an atmosphere of almost insuperable danger, coming from a number of strange and imaginative sources. Yet in some ways everything that follows is anticlimax. For much of *The Two Towers* people seem to be riding hither and yon on horseback to no great purpose, and at the climax of *Return of the King* Sauron's defeat is accomplished all too swiftly and easily: the dissipation of the great menace, built up through hundreds of pages, is encompassed in a couple of paragraphs. Each volume is shorter than its predecessor, too, which gives an unfortunate feeling of falling away.

And it is true that as the menace of Sauron is made explicit, when the hobbits return to the Shire and find awful changes made, it is of less than epic scope:

The pleasant row of old hobbit-holes in the bank on the north side of the Pool were deserted, and their little gardens that used to run bright to the water's edge were rank with weeds. Worse, there was a whole line of the ugly new houses all along Pool Side, where the Hobbiton Road ran close to the bank. An avenue of trees had stood there. They were all gone. And looking with dismay up the road towards Bag End they saw a tall chimney of brick in the distance. It was pouring out black smoke into the evening air.

There seems little doubt about what has happened here: the Industrial Revolution has come to the Shire, which is turning into something possibly resembling Birmingham. Luckily the hobbits, having succeeded in their

Opposite: *At Cirith Gorgor, the Haunted Pass, the Men of Gondor built great towers, to prevent Sauron returning to Mordor. But their vigilance lapsed, and Sauron rose again, and the Teeth of Mordor became his watch-towers.*

quest, are able to reverse the malign trend, and everything is restored to normality, more or less.

Of course, so immersed can one be in Tolkien's epic by this time that this does not seem particularly diminishing, and certainly does not seem odd. In Middle Earth factory chimneys are indeed out of place. The problem lies if one tries to extend this argument to the real world – as Tolkien did not, explicitly, though when he makes his feelings so clear there is no cause for complaint if readers do. Because Middle Earth never existed, and certainly pre-Industrial England was nothing like it. This is indeed backward-yearning, as Moorcock put it, but it is yearning backward to a mythical past.

But *The Lord of the Rings* nevertheless manages to transcend its weaknesses and rise above its critics. Tolkien may, as a person, have had all or none of the traits with which Moorcock brands him. It does not matter: we do not, in general, enjoy any kind of art on account of the opinions of its creator. What we judge is the creation. Here Ursula Le Guin, who encountered Tolkien as a mature adult, puts the crucial point most elegantly: "No ideologues, not even religious ones, are going to be happy with Tolkien, unless they manage it by misreading him. For like all great artists he escapes ideology by being too quick for its nets, too complex for its grand simplicities, too fantastic for its rationality, too real for its generalizations. They will no more keep Tolkien labelled and pickled in a bottle than they will *Beowulf*, or the *Elder Edda*, or the *Odyssey*."

After the publication of *The Lord of the Rings* Tolkien continued to work on *The Silmarillion*, whose appearance was more and more eagerly anticipated. Yet it must have been increasingly apparent that in fact he never would complete it, left to his own devices, for to finish it would be to put an end, in his mind, to Middle Earth, and Middle Earth had been part of his life for over 50 years. Only after his death could it be said to be completed, and be put in shape for publication.

The Silmarillion, unlike *The Hobbit* and *The Lord of the Rings*, is not a novel. It is a series of prose epics: the stories which the inhabitants of Middle Earth might pass down from one generation to the next. The language is incantatory, almost Biblical in places, and the tales span many years and generations. There are many paragraphs beginning "And it came to pass ..." or "It is told that ..." It is full of names of people and places and occurrences. But there are no characters, none of the small-scale detail which enables a reader to participate in the events and vicariously experience them. In this manner of telling, what happens in the three volumes of *The Lord of the Rings* occupies about half a page. *The Silmarillion* is without doubt evidence of a great deal of imaginative creation, but unlike Tolkien's previous books it is not – to borrow a piece of computer jargon – user friendly. It is quite probable that as well as being the best-selling hardback work of fiction ever, it is also among the least read. It may have been essential for Tolkien to do this work if he was to make Middle Earth real in his novels, but it is not necessary for us, his readers, to wish to share in his background research unless our interest in his creation becomes of academic intensity.

Like all successful writers Tolkien has attracted imitators. But he has done more. The success of *The Lord of the Rings* is not the only factor in the establishment of fantasy as one of the most popular modern forms of writing, but it is certainly the most significant factor. Robert E. Howard, too, was a major influence at the more action-oriented end of the spectrum, but it was Tolkien who opened the way for such later writers as Stephen Donaldson and Terry Brooks (whose best-selling *Sword of Shannara* is in effect a re-creation of *The Lord of the Rings*). Nowadays bookshops are packed with tales of wizards and elves and trolls and dragons, but few of them approach even remotely Tolkien's success. A fantasy novel is not difficult to write – indeed, in many ways its shape is pre-determined – but to create a fantasy world with such depth of detail is another matter. To do that you need to be sufficiently devoted to, and obsessed with, your creation to spend many years – even a lifetime – on it, as Tolkien did.

Chapter Two

LOST WORLDS

Illustrated by

Bill Donohue

"Creeping to his side, we looked over the rocks. The place into which we gazed was a pit, and may, in the early days, have been one of the smaller volcanic blow-holes of the plateau. It was bowl-shaped, and at the bottom, some hundreds of yards from where we lay, were pools of green-scummed, stagnant water, fringed with bull-rushes. It was a weird place in itself, but its occupants made it seem like a scene from the Seven Circles of Dante. The place was a rookery of pterodactyls. There were hundreds of them congregated within view. All the bottom area round the water-edge was alive with their young ones, and with hideous mothers brooding upon their leathery, yellowish eggs. From this crawling, flapping mass of obscene reptile life came the shocking clamour which filled the air and the mephitic, horrible, musty odour which turned us sick. But above, perched each upon its own stone, tall, grey, and withered, more like dead and dried specimens than actual living creatures, sat the horrible males, absolutely motionless save for the rolling of their red eyes or an occasional snap of their rat-trap beaks as a dragon-fly went past them. Their huge membranous wings were closed by folding their fore-arms, so that they sat like gigantic old women, wrapped in hideous web-coloured shawls, and with their ferocious heads protruding above them. Large and small, not less than a thousand of these filthy creatures lay in the hollow before us."

Sir Arthur Conan Doyle
THE LOST WORLD

There was a time when to talk of a "mysterious, lost valley" was to talk of that valley beyond the mountains to the east; you would never visit that remote land, because your family group, your tribe, was migrating northwards, and you were among the earliest of men.

Later, tales of lost worlds, or hidden civilisations, always placed those strange lands beyond the sailing scope of your fleetest ship, or further than your pack-animals could trek: thus, Atlantis could never be proved or disproved to the Mycenaeans who, perhaps, fantasised about the remote continent; and the heartlands of Africa, or the high mountains north of Constantinople, were places that hid dark, or bright secrets. Gold, of course, littered the ground like pebbles; beasts were fabulous; the rewards for the lucky travellers who could journey so far would be endless.

By the sixteenth century the world had shrunk to a much smaller place; there was a fabled treasure in the mountains of the New World, a city made of gold, and the Spanish proved that, with such riches as these as their goal, no lost world was safe from them. Even so, well until the late nineteenth century, more of the planet – the heartlands, the high-lands, the islands of storm-shrouded oceans – was unknown to the West than known, and the expectation of the discovery of wondrous things and landscapes remained high.

However, as new lands were opened, as the dark forests were unlocked, as the basalt cliffs of oceanic islands were scaled and their virgin landscapes explored, nothing was found but the old, and the primitive. There were no fabulous beasts, no lost civilisations, no crystal-towered castles, hidden from the gaze of man for thousands of years.

All this changed in the early years of this century, when two exotic discoveries were made, whose stories are now well known.

A young journalist, Edward Malone, in an

Preceding pages: The approach to the base of the huge plateau of Maple White Land: the crags above George Challenger and his party curve outwards at the top, so that direct ascent is out of the question.

attempt to win "fair lady" by participating in an expedition of high adventure, gate-crashed the house of a then eminent zoologist, who had recently returned from the Amazon basin with a remarkable discovery, following a solitary expedition of two years. In the words of the editor of Malone's newspaper, the man had "undoubtedly been to South America, but refused to say exactly where ... Something wonderful happened, or the man's a champion liar..."

The zoologist had reported seeing "queer animals", but had since retracted the statement, and refused all interviews. In fact, he regarded journalists as being a singularly offensive species of sub-human. The man was, of course, Professor George Challenger, larger than life in build, reputation and intellect, a man whose behaviour, way of working, and treatment of his fellow humans was considered quite scandalous in scientific circles of the day.

Despite the "obvious inferiority", Challenger saw Malone to possess "a glimmer of intelligence" and to be clearly well along the evolutionary line that would one day lead to the fully human species of which the Professor himself was the sole existing representative. Thus Malone gained the man's confidence and was apprised of the finer details of that earlier expedition, details which were in the form of sketches, a blurred photograph, and notes made by a previous explorer, Maple White, whom Challenger had found dead in a remote Indian village. "There were indications as to the direction from which the dead traveller had come ... [Challenger's words] ... but Indian legends alone would have been my guide, for I found that rumours of a strange land were common among the riverine tribes". The Indians, it seems lived in dread of "Curupuri". "Curupuri is the spirit of the woods, something terrible, something malevolent, something to be avoided. None can describe its shape or nature, but it is a word of terror along the Amazon."

Maple White had made a painting of that frightening place: It was a full page sketch of a landscape roughly tinted in colour...There was a pale-green foreground of feathery vegetation, which sloped upwards and ended in a line of cliffs dark red in colour, and curiously ribbed like some basaltic formations... They extended in an unbroken wall right across the background. At one point was an isolated pyramidal rock, crowned by a great tree, which appeared to be separated by a cleft from the main crag. Behind it all, a blue tropical sky.

But what did this picture prove? Challenger explained his own theory, and Malone gained the first hint of the dramatic discovery that Challenger and Maple White had made. South America is a granitic continent. At this particular place in the interior, in some far distant age, there had been a great, sudden volcanic upheavel. The cliffs shown in the painting were basaltic and antideluvian. An area, perhaps as large as Sussex, had been lifted up *en bloc* with all its living contents, and been cut off by perpendicular precipices of a hardness which had defied erosion from all the rest of the continent. The result? The ordinary laws of nature were suspended; creatures survived which would otherwise have disappeared. The plateau that surmounted those cliffs was a world, lost from its own time, isolated from ours...

The rest of the story is familiar. The second expedition, including the intrepid Malone and led by the practically impossible Professor Challenger, struck out for the plateau a year or so later, and after much hardship scaled the cliffs and discovered the archaic land that existed upon it, a place where dinosaurs competed with primitive forms of man for the limited territory, and a food supply that consisted largely of extinct species of mammals, such as the giant elk and armadillo. This diet was supplemented by fish from the vast lake sited in the centre of the plateau:

It boiled and heaved with strange life. Great slate-coloured backs and high serrated dorsal fins shot up with a fringe of silver, then rolled down to the depths again. The sandbanks were spotted with uncouth crawling forms, huge turtles, strange saurians, and one great flat creature like a writhing, palpitating mat of black greasy leather, which flopped its way slowly to the lake. Here and there high serpent heads projected out of the water, cutting swiftly through it with a little collar of foam in front, and a long swirling wake behind, rising and falling in graceful, swanlike undulations as they went.

This was a description that astonished a sceptical, scientific world: the description of a fresh-water plesiosaurus! But in the weeks that the expedition spent upon the plateau, stranger, more marvellous sights were seen: from a great community of pterodactyls, living in the crater of an extinct volcano, to herds of grazing iguanodons and the aftermath of an attack on such a herd by giant sabre-toothed tigers.

The complete adventure was recorded by Arthur Conan Doyle as *The Lost World*.

A few years later, almost exactly on the opposite side of the globe, another strange tale of a lost world began to be unfolded. Written down as *Lost Horizon*, by James Hilton, it tells the story of the discovery of Shangri-la, a fertile, populated valley hidden away in the remote Tibetan mountains, and watched over by the lamasery, where the monks were guardians of an astonishing secret.

There seemed to be a tradition in the early part of this century that tales of exploration and discovery could never be narrated straight. A lot of the fun, a great deal of the entertainment of the books, comes in the *way* that clues as to the lost places are discovered. Old manuscripts, messages in bottles, stories told to people, then to others, and finally to the adventurer, and so forth. Remember how Professor Lidenbrock realised that there was a pathway down to the centre of the Earth? He discovered a sixteenth-century parchment written in Latin but with the letters coded into Icelandic Runes:

Descend into the crater of Sneffells Yokul, over which the shadow of Scartaris falls, before the kalends of July, bold traveller, and you will reach the centre of the earth. I have done this. Arne Saknussem.

In *Lost Horizon*, a group of old school friends, Rutherford, Wyland, Aanders and Hilton, get together for a chat. During the evening, mention is made of a British Consul (Hugh Conway) who was aboard a plane, with a party of men and women, which disappeared some years before. A "very rum affair". Rutherford, though, is very disturbed by something, and later confides to Hilton that he has *seen* the lost Conway quite recently. He tells Hilton how. It transpires that Rutherford was travelling on a train to Shanghai and got into conversation with a nun from a mission at Chiang-King. She had an unusual case of fever at the mission, and Rutherford, visiting the mission on a stop-over recognised the long lost Conway. Conway recovered, but had lost his memory. However, he played two Chopin piano studies that are unknown. He had learned them from "one who studied with Chopin", even though the composer died a hundred years before. At last, Conway's memory returned and he told Rutherford his strange story, and Rutherford had written it down, and gives it to Hilton to read, and after all this the *real* story begins.

The word convoluted could have been invented for that introduction. Nevertheless, the story that follows is magic, involving the deliberate abduction of Conway and his companions, and their transport into the mountainous regions of the Tibetan heartlands. Confused, angry, slightly frightened, Conway is nevertheless awed by the majestic landscape across which he is flown:

Then he turned to the window and gazed out. The surrounding sky had cleared completely, and in the light of late afternoon there came to him a vision which, for an instant, snatched the remaining breath out of his lungs. Far away, at the very limit of dis-

Preceding pages: *"A group of coloured pavilions clung to the mountainside with none of the deliberation of a Rhineland Castle, but rather with the chance delicacy of flower-petals impaled upon a crag." In the distance, blocking in the lost valley, is the mountain Karakal.*

tance, lay range upon range of snow-peaks, festooned with glaciers, and floating, in appearance, upon vast levels of cloud. They compassed the whole arc of the circle, merging towards the west in a horizon that was fierce, almost garish in colouring... And meanwhile the plane, on that stupendous stage, was droning over an abyss in face of a sheer white wall that seemed part of the sky itself until the sun caught it. Then ... it flamed into superb and dazzling incandescence.

All fear drains from Conway as he is steeped in the majesty and remoteness of this utterly deserted landscape ("Gee, what scenery," is the only comment made by the American on board). They are flying into the twilight, across a land that has never been explored, mainly because the peaks, not being the highest in the world, attract no need of conquest, like Everest. "The peaks had a chill gleam; utterly majestic and remote, their very namelessness had dignity". When twilight falls, a full moon rises, "touching each peak in succession like some celestial lamplighter, until the long horizon glittered against a blue-black sky".

Thus, with vivid prose, the reader is taken chillingly far from civilisation, sharing Conway's sense of remoteness from the familiar clutter of the lowland cities and towns. This is a land that he had often thought about as being unexplored, but had never conceived of as being so *vast*. It sets the reader up wonderfully for the haunting solitariness of the lamasery that is eventually found, hidden away in a verdant valley amongst this vast spread of desolate nature.

The party are approaching the lost valley along a steep mountains path, and the downward prospect is terrifying, the descent into the valley itself. The buildings of the monastery cling to sheer walls, near the top of the mountain, but the mountain wall continues to drop, "nearly perpendicular, into a cleft that could only have been the result of some cataclysm in the far past". Conway can see the floor of the valley, hazily distant, a welcome patch of greenness in the snow wastes. The valley is protected by sheer walls, unscalable ranges, although there is a precipitous pathway from the lamasery to the landlocked valley below. The lamasery "observes" the valley, rather than dominates it; the valley, rather, is dominated by the huge mountain of Karakal, blue-topped and silent; it seems very threatening to Conway; beyond that mountain is an immense glacier, and only Karakal stands between that immense wall of ice and the tiny oasis of green. Sometimes it seems as if the whole valley shakes with the shuddering strain of rock versus ice. At times, during the year, huge storms rack the valley, and the people who live there believe them to be sent by demons, raging beyond the mountain walls. The valley is cut off from space, and time, and time has slowed. The inhabitants, looked after by the monks who occupy the lamasery, have no conception of the world beyond the valley, imagining that the mountains stretch forever, inhabited by wandering unfortunates who occasionally find their way to "the world".

All who live there are practically immortal. The young are old, the old are timeless. After thousands of years, the timeless pass on, and this is what is happening to the High Lama. But this most old of men has had a vision of a New Dark Age, the war that will devastate the world. In Conway he has found a son to whom he can confide his vision, and entrust the knowledge of the valley. Conway must come to the valley, the youngest of them, the most vigorous. He must replace the dying Lama.

It's a smashing story, let down, these days, only by its awful Englishness ("I say old boy, this chap's a jolly rum fellow, what?").

The attraction of the "lost realm", the valley or plateau cut off from the normal flow of civilisation, remains strong. It flourished as a fictive genre at a time when the world was almost totally explored, and the romance of the real explorers was waning as the only wonders accumulated were zoological and botanical ones – only! For the lost realms of the fabulous, then, the reader turned to fiction, where those remaining outposts of unexplored territory could still be invested with wonder. Lost worlds, lost races, lost cities featured strongly in the imaginative fiction of the late 19th and early 20th centuries. They replaced that "fantastic journey" as a favourite form, now that so much of the world was charted and explored, and writers such as H. Rider Haggard exploited the romantic idea of a mysterious, hidden civilisation to the full. Haggard is the undisputed master: *King Solomon's Mines*, *Allan Quartermain* and *She* are marvellous blends of geographical accuracy and seductive fantasy as intrepid white explorers find the remnants of exotic civilisations – a store of diamonds, a bizarre and astonishingly beautiful priestess: *She who must be obeyed.*

Rider Haggard was imitated, but never matched. He wrote other novels on the lost race theme, *The People of the Mist* and *Queen Sheba's Ring*, for example, but none are as good as the first three. In imitation of Haggard some fine adventures were produced. Edgar Rice Burroughs constantly had his most popular hero, Tarzan of the Apes, discovering lost races and tribes in the African jungles. He also wrote *The Land that Time Forgot*, in the vein of Conan Doyle's *The Lost World*, and *At the Earth's Core*, which used one location which, whilst being "lost", was also stretching credibility: the imagined hollow earth. Jules Verne's *Journey to the Centre of the Earth* does it best, with his three heroes descending via an extinct volcano, to find that the inside of the earth is not molten, but cool, crystalline, mysterious. The centre of the world is in a gigantic sea. Prehistoric monsters and sunken cities are among their fantastic discoveries.

Abraham Merritt and Dennis Wheatley contributed to the genre, Merritt with *Dwellers in the Mirage* and *The Face in the Abyss* and Wheatley with *The Fabulous Valley* and *The Man who Missed the War*. More recently, Garry Kilworth and Richard Cowper have shown that a "tingle" of awe can still be gleaned from the idea of discovering that which has been hidden from modern eyes. Kilworth's "Blind Windows" takes the search for a fourth primary colour into the heart of a mountain and the ancient culture of man-forms that live there. Cowper's "The Web of the Magi" has echoes of *The Lost Horizon*. High in the mountains of Persia an explorer finds a fertile valley, a strange yet welcoming community, and an immense tapestry being woven on a gigantic loom. The tapestry symbolises the progress of the human species, but the greatest tapestry is the mental one that fills the surrounding mountain and into which the explorer is drawn – here, as he plays with time and space, so he *affects* reality. Even primal woodlands hide strange lost worlds. Robert Holdstock's "Mythago Wood" is an oak woodland that has "defended" itself against man since the last Ice Age. It is the home of lost characters and creatures of legend, and the deeper one penetrates the forest, the wilder and more bizarre that hidden land becomes. Finally, in a recent film, *The Valley: Obscured by Clouds*, young travellers winde their way to the highlands of Papua, New Guinea, to find a valley which cannot be seen from the air because of the cloud cover: the wildest part of the Earth, where in the 1950s the indigenous populations were a stable, stone-age hunter-gatherer society, at the bow-and-arrow level of technology, even that remote wilderness needed cloud cover to avoid the possibility that satellites could have monitored its secrets from space.

What lost lands can now remain? The Amazon Basin has given up its secrets; the heart of Africa is no longer a dark mystery; Australia is a wasteland, but without magic; New Guinea has a thriving tourist trade watching its stone-age culture learning to ride rough-track motorcyles. Beneath the polar ice-caps remains a shivery possible location for some long lost civilisation. Parts of remote Canada and Alaska, parts of China, these remain possible scenarios for the discovery of the unexpected. But the most exciting unknown world remains shrouded not just in geographical remoteness, but in political remoteness, a plateau or a lost valley hidden from western eyes not by sheer walls of basalt, but by an equally impenetrable curtain of iron.

The Soviet Union is a landscape of unimaginable vastness and desolation. It is too easy to forget that what we think of as "Russia" is an area which, to the USSR, is as Kent to the United Kingdom. And from the Caucasus in the west (which is to say, between the Black and Caspian seas) to the Tien Shan

and Pamur mountains, onwards to the Altai mountains of Mongolia is an immense expanse of hostile, unknown terrain. "Wild men" were recorded as inhabiting this area in mediaeval times. In the 1920s there were several encounters with creatures, half man, half ape, especially in the Altai mountains in South western Mongolia. One, even, was shot and buried beneath a cairn of stones. As is wont to happen in the villages of remote places, stories of encounters with troglodytes abound: the yeti, the bigfoot, wolf-children, hermits...

Who knows what part of the human psyche is responsible for creating such fearsome, wild inhabitants of any land that is difficult to penetrate, and who knows what *genuine* descendants of earlier forms of the human species remain, isolated and flourishing in those vast wastes? We talk of "relics", of "primitive creatures", of survivals from an earlier age. But there are no "survivals". There are no "relics". Any culture – call it Homo sapiens *neanderthalensis* if you will – that exists today is *modern*. In the same way that the so-called "stone-age" inhabitants of New Guinea can grasp any concept that you and I can grasp, and adapt to 20th century living with as much ease as a child growing into a technological society so *any* group or tribe of creatures that represents the modern equivalent of an earlier form of man are the product of the same span of evolutionary time, the same passage of generations, the same non-selective cognitive sophistication that we may have enjoyed!

If there *are* Neanderthals in the remote hills of Mongolia, they will not be living fossils. They will, nonetheless, be a richer treasure than any gold, or Saurian left-over, or magic process that the human mind can wildly imagine. And they will be the most fragile of treasures, for their true value will be in the fact of their existence, known, but mostly unobserved, briefly contacted, and then left to their own devices.

The frustrating truth of the matter is this: the realms of fantasy that are lost worlds must remain a fiction; because any real lost world, discovered by the present generation of Homo sapiens, will rapidly become folklore.

Chapter Three

GORMENGHAST
The Realm of Titus Groan

Illustrated by

Ian Miller

"Gormenghast, that is, the main massing of the original stone, taken by itself would have displayed a certain ponderous architectural quality were it possible to have ignored the circumfusion of those mean dwellings that swarmed like an epidemic around its Outer Walls. They sprawled over the sloping earth, each one halfway over its neighbour until, held back by the castle ramparts, the innermost of these hovels laid hold on the Great Walls, clamping themselves thereto like limpets to a rock... Over their irregular roofs would fall, throughout the seasons, the shadow of time-eaten buttresses, of broken and lofty turrets, and, most enormous of all, the shadow of the Tower of Flints. This tower, patched unevenly with black ivy, arose like a mutilated finger from among the fists of knuckled masonry and pointed blasphemously at heaven. At night the owls made of it an echoing throat; by day it stood voiceless and cast its long shadow."

Mervyn Peake
TITUS GROAN

There can be no better intro-duction to the extraordinary world of Gormenghast than that provided by author Mervyn Peake on the first page of *Titus Groan*, first published in 1946. His dense and vivid prose establishes in this single paragraph a number of interlocking images which foreshadow what is to come. There is the ancient, crumbling immensity of Gormenghast, with its "time-eaten buttres-ses", its ivy-clad and broken towers. There is the Gothic sense of menace: a tower like a muti-lated finger, pointed blasphemously at heaven and the night-time haunt of owls, is not likely to be the scene of peaceful goings-on. Above all there is the image of the castle almost as a living being, a stone Leviathan heaving itself above the ground, with lesser dwellings clinging to its immense sides like parasites.

As the novel progresses the aptness of this latter image becomes more and more apparent, for while *Titus Groan* and its successors (*Gormenghast* and *Titus Alone*) are thronged with strange, bizarre and memorable characters, it is the castle itself whose huge, brooding presence dominates all. Nor is it especially fanciful to see an analogy between Gormenghast the castle and the *Gormenghast* trilogy: as the former dominates its landscape so the latter towers over the terrain of Gothic fantasy, making other such novels seem puny and mean by comparison. There is no other book remotely to rival Peake's achievement.

Mervyn Peake was a man of many talents: illustrator and painter, set designer, novelist, poet and playwright. He was born in China in 1911, but returned to England with his parents while still a boy. He first made his reputation as an illustrator – both of classics like *The Hunting of the Snark* and *Alice in Wonder-land*, and of his own works, such as *Captain Slaughterboard Drops Anchor* – and today any book illustrated by Peake is a collector's item. He served in the Army during the Second

Opposite: The Tower of Flints was inhabited largely by owls – but also, later, by Sepulchrave, Earl of Groan who, with the cook Swelter, was devoured by them.

World War, firstly in the Engineers, but later as an official war artist; in the latter capacity he was one of the first people from outside to witness the horrors of Belsen concentration camp, an experience reflected particularly in *Titus Alone*.

He began writing *Titus Groan* while still in the Army, lugging the manuscript around in his kitbag. He had completed a substantial proportion of the novel when the manuscript was lost; Peake, undaunted, started again from the beginning, and the novel was published the year after the war ended.

The novel generally accepted to have founded the sub-genre of Gothic fiction is Horace Walpole's *The Castle of Otranto* (1764). Walpole – son of the first British Prime Minister – originally published the novel pseudonymously, pretending it to be the translation of an Italian manuscript. It is a melodramatic tale of villainy and revenge, with supernatural trimmings (most famously a gigantic armoured helm which falls out of nowhere, crushing to death one of the characters). Immensely successful, it started a vogue for novels of this sort, which began to appear in profusion (Jane Austen's *North-anger Abbey* parodies the genre). The horror writer H. P. Lovecraft characterised the Gothic fantasy's milieu succinctly: "This novel dramatic paraphernalia consisted first of all of the Gothic castle, with its awesome antiquity, vast distances and ramblings, deserted or ruined wings, damp corridors, unwholesome hidden catacombs, and galaxy of ghosts and appalling legends, as a nucleus of suspense and daemoniac fright ... the infinite array of stage properties includes strange lights, damp trap-doors, extinguished lamps, mouldy hidden manuscripts, creaking hinges, shaking arras, and the like."

Up to a point this description fits Gor-menghast well enough, but there is an import-ant difference which sets Peake's trilogy apart from the general run of Gothic fantasy. There is no supernatural element in his books: no ghosts, no giant helmets falling from the sky. Instead Peake creates an imaginary world, an entire Gothic realm, as the setting for his books. The world of Gormenghast has no

connections with our own: it is not in our past, or our future, or somewhere forgotten off the end of the map. It is simply *other*. For this reason it belongs alongside the other invented fantasy worlds of this book.

When *Titus Groan* begins, the character for whom the novel is named is not yet born; indeed, by the end of the book he is only two years old. But though he does not start to play an active part as a character until the second novel of the trilogy, Titus is the focus from the beginning. His birth sets into creaking motion one more set of the wheels of ritual which govern everything in Gormenghast; and as these unfold so too do the rivalries and plots and intrigues which the book describes.

Gormenghast is ancient and unchanging. Its current Lord, Sepulchrave, like his predecessors, has every waking minute mapped out for him. His Librarian, Sourdust, comes to him each morning as Sepulchrave sits in front of an immense breakfast which will go largely uneaten, carrying four books in which the rituals are enshrined. At precisely twenty minutes to ten each morning Sepulchrave summons Sourdust to his side and they begin the plan the day, opening the first book:

> The left-hand pages were headed with the date and ... this was followed by a list of the activities to be performed hour by hour during the day by his Lordship. The exact times, the garments to be worn for each occasion, and the symbolic gestures to be used. Diagrams facing the left-hand page gave particulars of the routes by which his Lordship should approach the various scenes of operation.

Into this unchanging world are introduced characters who will oppose this oppressive

Preceding pages: *The Hall of Bright Carvings occupies the top storey of the north wing of Gormenghast. Here Rottcodd looked after the choicest carvings - the Emerald Horse, the piebald Shark - dusting them by the light of seven great candelabra which were never extinguished, and allowing the dust to collect in drifts on the floor.*

obsession with tradition. There is Titus himself, but chiefly in the first novel there is Steerpike, who begins as a humble kitchen assistant, but who through devious machinations - and murder - rises to a position of power (and eventually, in *Gormenghast*, into confrontation with Titus).

We initially encounter Steerpike in the Great Kitchen of Gormenghast, in the first of the many brilliant descriptive set-pieces which stud the novel. The kitchen is a bedlam of heat, noise and drunkenness, presided over by the bloated and vulgar chef, Swelter. So vast is the room that a company of eighteen men, known as the Grey Scrubbers, are required to keep its grey stone walls and floor clean - men descended from families whose hereditary duty it has been for so long that they have become very like grey slabs of stone themselves. An array of huge ovens produces a stream of food which is borne away to distant parts of the castle.

Steerpike is virtually the only character in the novel who could really be described as normal, which gives his later actions an ambiguous tone. One of Peake's other great strengths is in his creation of a whole series of unforgettable characters: people who are not so much larger than life, but rather enlarge life to fit their generous proportions. There is Lord Sepulchrave and Swelter; there is Flay, the Lord's servant, whose knee-joints perpetually crack as he walks; there is the immense, bed-ridden Countess Groan; there is the cackling Dr Prunesquallor and his vain sister Irma. In this aspect, particularly, of his work, Peake has frequently and with reason been compared with Charles Dickens, whose characters similarly magnify life. As Michael Moorcock put it: "What gives the *Gormenghast* books their power and quality is not so much their fantastic elements as their characters ... who have bizarre names, certainly, but are as alive and credible as Dickens's finest creations. And it is with Dickens alone that Mervyn Peake can be compared. No other writer since Dickens has had the energy, the invention, the powers of observation, the capacity for rich and brilliant metaphor or the skill to control the flood of original invention, for one of Peake's most remarkable qualities was his craftsman-ship, his control over the creations of his unique imagination."

And, like Dickens, Peake is also a *comic* writer, in the best sense. Humour in fantasy is not a common attribute. There are few laughs in Tolkien, for instance. Genuine comedy is not simply a matter of cracking jokes; instead, it proceeds from real perception of character. Most of the characters of fantasy tend to the archetypal; Peake's are highly individual comic grotesques. When some awful fate befalls them it therefore affects us more strongly than if a noble but cardboard hero has met a noble end.

The world outside Gormenghast is domin-ated by its presence. The people are known as the Mud or Clay Dwellers; their mean hovels are crowded together and no more than eight feet high. The central ritual of their lives is the production of the Bright Carvings – strange, grotesque representations of figures or animals. Once a year they are admitted to the castle grounds, and the Earl of Groan selects the best of the Carvings. These are taken into Gormenghast, to the Hall of the Bright Carvings, where they are promptly forgotten by everybody except Rottcodd, their curator. A more pathetic and pointless kind of serfdom would be hard to imagine.

But for all its other qualities it is, as we have said, Gormenghast itself which is the main character of *Titus Groan*. As he takes us around the castle Peake conjures scene after scene with a painter's vivid eye and a writer's sure choice of words. There is, for instance, the Stone Hall, where Lord Sepulchrave takes his breakfast:

On either side and running the entire length, great pillars prop the painted ceiling where cherubs pursue each other across a waste of flaking sky. There must be about a thousand of them all told, interweaving among the clouds, their fat limbs forever on the move and yet never moving, for they are imperfectly articulated. The colours, once garish, have faded and peeled away and the ceiling is now a very subtle shade of grey and lichen green, old rose and silver.

Or there is the vast roofscape of Gor-menghast, a "field of flagstones", as viewed by Steerpike:

When Steerpike began his scrutiny the roofscape was neither more nor less than a conglomeration of stone structures spread-ing to right and left and away from him. It was a mist of masonry. As he peered, taking each structure individually, he found that he was a spectator of a stationary gathering of stone personalities... He had seen, growing from three-quarters the way up a sheer, windowless face of otherwise arid wall, a tree that curved out and upward, dividing and subdividing until a labyrinth of twigs gave to its contour a blur of sunlit smoke. The tree was dead, but having grown from the south side of the wall it was shielded from the violence of the winds, and judging by the harmonious fanlike beauty of its shape, it had not suffered the loss of a single sapless limb. Upon the lit wall its perfect shadow lay as though engraved with superhuman skill.

The novel is full of such descriptions: the Hall of the Bright Carvings, the Attic, the Library, the Room of Roots, the Hall of Spiders. It reaches its climax with the long battle between Flay and Swelter, at the end of which the obese cook is slain, only for Lord Sepulchrave – who has by this time, been driven completely insane by the burning of his beloved Library – to appear and claim the body for the owls with whom he shares the Tower of Flints. The scene which follows is as memorably horrific as anything in modern literature:

Of the nightmare that followed it is needful to say only that long hours of toil culminated at the Tower of Flints to which they had dragged the body, after having steered it between a gap in the battlements through which the lake was emptying itself. Swelter had descended in the two-hundred-feet cascade of moon-sparkling water and they had found his body, spread to the size of a sheet and bubbling on the drenched gravel. A rope had been procured and a hook

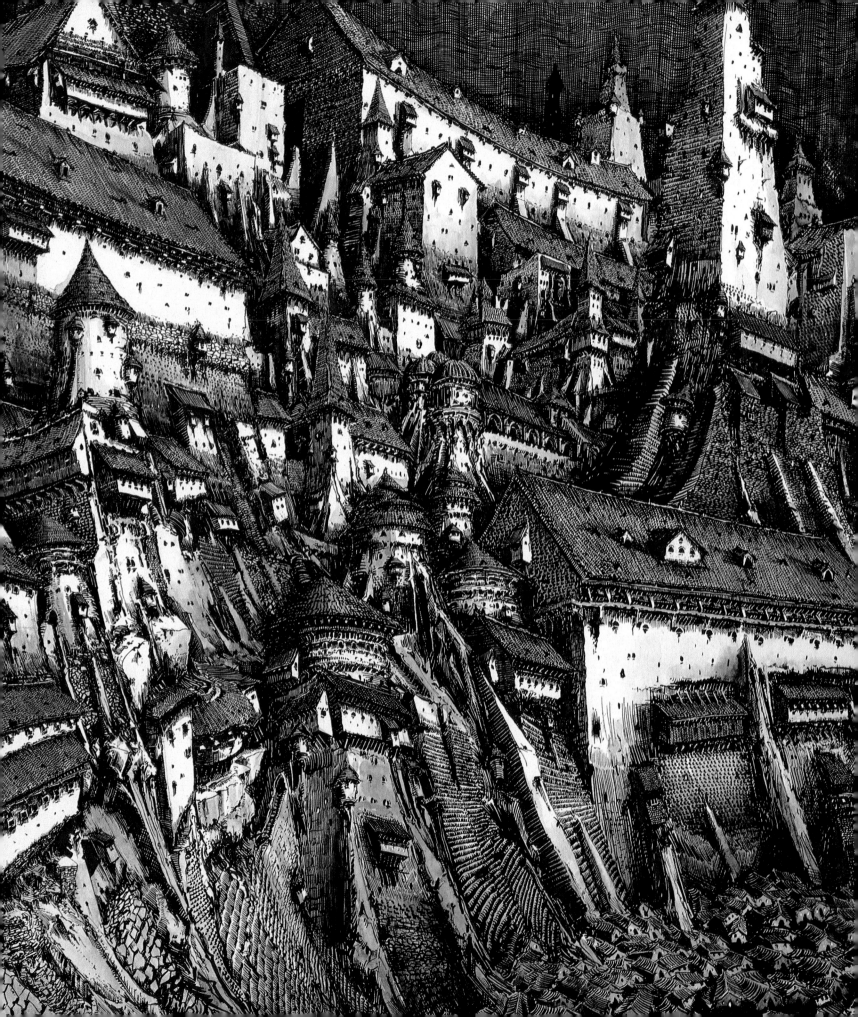

attached and the long drag had at last been effected.

The white silence was terrible. The moonlight like a hoar frost on the Tower of Flints. The shell of the library glimmered in the distance far down the long line of halls and pavilions, and of domed, foresaken structures. To their right the lit pinewoods were split with lines of midnight. About their feet a few cones, like ivory carvings, were scattered, anchored to the pale earth by their shadows.

What was once Swelter glistened.

The discussion in this chapter has largely centred on *Titus Groan*, the first book of the trilogy, for it is here that the castle itself is introduced and explored at length, and our main concern is with the worlds created by fantasy writers. Among these Gormenghast is virtually unique: a portrait of a building so immense, convoluted and labyrinthine in its architecture that it comes almost to represent a bizarre model of the human brain itself. Perhaps the nearest approach to it is to be found in *Gloriana* (1978), a novel by Peake's friend and admirer Michael Moorcock, which is dedicated to his memory. In an appreciation he wrote after Peake's death Moorcock said: "Mervyn would have been humorously embarrassed if one had called him a seminal figure to his face, but there is no doubting the influence that he has had on a large number of young writers, perhaps even more from the point of view of subject matter and technique than of style. His outlook certainly had a considerable influence on what I think is my best work, and some of my early stories were nothing less than imitations of the *Gormenghast* books."

But there is much to admire also in the other books. *Gormenghast* brings to a conclusion

Preceding pages: *Around the bulk of Gormenghast swarm the Clay Dwellings, whose inhabitants labour all year round to produce the Bright Carvings. Their crowded houses are dominated by the immense Castle, with its turrets and battlements - huge and brooding, a crumbling citadel of stone.*

Opposite: *The Tree, now dead but undamaged by decay, grew out from the side of a tower. Steerpike could see two figures walking along the main stem: the sisters Cora and Clarice, who reached the tree through the Room of Roots, where every tendril of root had been lovingly hand painted by the sisters, in seven colours - a task that took three years to complete.*

Steerpike's story and at the end Titus, still a boy, abandons the castle for the world outside. The third book, *Titus Alone*, shows us something of that world - which is not unlike our own - but the picture, while powerful in parts, is fragmentary, and the novel a shadow of its predecessors, for in 1958, while working the book, Mervyn Peake developed encephalitis - a severe brain infection whose affects are akin to those of Parkinson's Disease - and for the last decade of his life was unable to work. The novel was pieced together from his manuscripts, but cannot be regarded as complete. (The version published in 1959 was superseded, in 1970, by an edition more faithful to the author's apparent intentions). Had Peake been able to continue working there would evidently have been a fourth volume as well, but the intended final shape of the work can only be a matter for conjecture.

That such a disease should afflict so energetic and creative a personality is particularly tragic. When he died, in 1968, Peake was only 57 years old, but his creative life had ended ten years earlier, when he should still have been in vigorous middle age. Like many true originals he initially attracted only a limited following, but over the years his unique books have become known and admired by an ever wider audience. C. S. Lewis said of them: "Mr Peake created a new category, the Gormenghastly, and we wonder already how we did without it and why no one defined it before." And novelist and critic Elizabeth Bowen said of *Titus Groan*: "One of those works of pure, violent, self-sufficient imagination that are from time to time thrown up." Peake's work owed nothing to fashion, little to any of his contemporaries, and not much to any predecessor.

Chapter Four

MARS

Illustrated by

Dan Woods

"He walked between two worlds. He went through valleys drowsing in the heat of the summer day, where leafy branches of strange trees raked his face and the juice of crushed grasses stained his sandals. Life, winged and furred and soft of foot, fled from him with a stir and a rustle. And yet he knew that he walked in a desert, where even the wind had forgotten the names of the dead for whom it mourned.

"He crossed high ridges, where the sea lay before him and he could hear the boom of the surf on the beaches. And yet he saw only a vast dead plain, where the dust ran in little wavelets among the dry reefs. The truths of thirty years' living are not easily forgotten."

Leigh Brackett
THE SWORD OF RHIANNON

Mars, perhaps because of its associations with war and fire, has always been the most appealing – even romantic – of the planets, and has long been the science fiction writers' favourite. Brilliant in the night sky, but a dazzling, blood red when seen at dawn, it is easy to see how the planet, linking with the religious and mystic beliefs of the day, has emerged as the heavenly symbol of things warlike, things strong, deeds conquering. While Venus dazzles, pearly white, and speaks of love and more gentle romance to the earth-bound observer, Mars is a bloodstained sword point, portending violence. The god, Mars, is always an armed man, sometimes mounted on a horse, carrying a lance or blade. In Mars are seen the virtues of courage and passion; it is associated with iron, the metal that has won Empires from the time of Christ. All this was attributed symbolically to a dry, sand-blasted world, which shivers at average temperatures below freezing point, as the cold of space reaches through a tenuous atmosphere only six thousandths as heavy as that of earth. No fire burns, and iron corrodes to red dust in a matter of hours.

If any work of fiction can be said to have "begun" the exploration of the Mars of the imagination, the world as a realm of fantasy, it is surely *The War of the Worlds*. Wells' sombre and haunting novel never visits the planet save by implication and contrast and, unlike the fantasists that followed, he attributed to the planet something of its real quality. He described the Martians peering from their icy, drying, decaying world, across the gulf of space, towards the sun, to earth, "a morning star of hope, our own warmer planet, green with vegetation and grey with water, with a cloudy atmosphere eloquent of fertility." The irony of the conquest that follows is that the "eloquent fertility" is transformed, by the invaders, into a wasteland of red weed, the staple food of the Martians, that spreads across the Earth until it, too, glows red at sunset.

Wells was fascinated by, if not in accord with, the extant belief in Mars as a world covered by dead seas and dried, ruined canals, an idea that had been proposed by Schiaparelli, and later taken up by Lowell. It's an image – that of a landscape criss-crossed by the bone-dry, vertically-sided remnants of great water-ways – that is too stirring to ever abandon. Even the landings of the Mariner spacecraft have not totally banished the haunting hope that somewhere, below the ice and dust that swirls in great storms above the vermilion land, the stone channels of that lost civilisation will still be found.

To some, at least, the real Mars – the planet as revealed by fly-bys then landings – is far more fascinating and dramatic than the imaginary world of the nineteenth century astronomers. If the planet is small and desolate, a huge desert strewn with rocks when seen from ground level, what a vista it must present to a vehicle travelling at just above that surface, with its huge, wind-scoured rifts and dried river beds, the imposing rise of the great volcano, Olympus Mons, the shimmering, scarped ice-caps, the surface snows of water and carbon dioxide raised into twisting ice sculptures, endlessly changing shape.

And this most real of Martian landscapes is creeping into fantasy already, for example Philip Farmer's *Jesus on Mars*, in which a human expedition tours the surface, and lands close to the gigantic rift known as the *Tithonius Chasm*:

> The great canyon complex of the *Valles Marineris* was a black wound on a red body. It ran for 3000 miles from east to west near the equator of Mars. At its widest it was fifty miles and at its deepest, several miles. If it resembled a terrible gash in a corpse, it also looked like a colossal centipede, the legs being the channels winding through the highlands towards the vast rift...
>
> The top of *Olympus Mons*, a volcano as wide as the state of New Mexico and 15.5 miles high, sank out of sight. The Tharsis Ridge, looking like a colossal dinosaur with fleshy dorsal plates, widened and then dropped out of sight.

In the words of a skilled writer, astronomy and exo-geology come alive. Farmer has sent his Marsnauts to investigate the hulking ruins of an ancient spaceship, whose curving hull is just emerging from a landslide, at the base of the chasm:

> Like a mouth, the rift opened beneath him. The vast mounds of the volcanos outside dropped, and presently the ship was below the edges of the awesomely towering cliffs. They were still in the thin but bright sunlight of the red planet. Not until the sun was low would the shadow of the western wall fall on them.

And thus the oldest, most romantic realm of fantasy enters the realm of fictional reality; the landscape, once so dense with red vegetation and ruins and darting creatures, retires to bleak, silent desert; the element of fantasy must be supplied by fragmentary remains of alien technology.

But the journey to this new reality has been complex, rich and fascinating in fiction, and in the hands of two writers at least, has established two alter egos of Mars that will never be forgotten.

Edgar Rice Burroughs was in his mid-thirties when he published, in 1912, his first short story, "Under the Moons of Mars". At that time Burroughs, a Westerner, had tried his hand at many jobs, from cowboy to teacher, railroad detective to soldier. Having read a story in an adventure magazine that was too awful for words, he decided that he could do a lot better. He certainly proved his point. His jungle hero Tarzan of the Apes is now, with Superman and Sherlock Holmes, one of the most famous men who never lived. But that first story of Burroughs', which set him on the road to multi-million sales of his books, concerned Mars, and a Mars as rich in jungle as the Africa of Tarzan would be, as populated by threatening natives and as rife with white princesses and slave traders as that same African territory would become. Called Barsoom, the Martian landscape which Burroughs created was that of Mars thousands of years ago, during the last days of the great civilisations whose waterways the astronomer, Lowell, saw as the ruined canals. To this weird and wonderful world goes John Carter, and the series of novels, from *Princess of Mars* through *Warlord of Mars, Fighting Men, Gods* etc *of Mars*, are among the most popular juvenile science fantasy read today.

John Carter is a professional adventurer, turned prospector, during the late eighteen hundreds. He is saved from certain death at the hands of Apaches by hiding in a cave, wherein time and space "slip". He finds himself abruptly standing on the moss-covered dead-sea bottom of a strange world, naked, alone, aware of the presence of gigantic creatures with green skins:

> Here were the great males towering in all the majesty of their imposing height; here were the gleaming white tusks protruding from their massive lower jaws to a point near the centre of their foreheads, the laterally placed, protruding eyes with which they could look forward or backward, or to either side without turning their heads, here the strange antennae-like ears rising from the tops of their foreheads; and the additional pair of arms extending from midway between the shoulders and the hips.

This is Barsoom, he discovers, Mars, thousands of years before his own time, a verdant, lush place, a planet whose landscape shifts from mossy wastes to dense jungles teaming with all manner of exotic alien life; cities hug gigantic cliffs, or sprawl around the grey oceans, where sea-going vessels ply their trade; immense airships, powered by barsoomian rays, drift over these cities, throwing down all sorts of fire. For all of this, Mars is a dying world, the atmosphere thinning, the warring races of green men, red men, blue men and all the other types of men, rapidly dying out as the oxygen is exhausted. This terrible fate has created chaos, and the planet, once a garden of Eden, is now a fiercely competitive jungle.

Part of the magic of Burroughs is that he wastes no time in getting you into the action, and does not then hesitate to recapitulate previous adventures, painting a word portrait of the world of Barsoom, and its manifold characters, in a few tight paragraphs. Here is how *Warlord of Mars* opens:

In the shadow of the forest that flanks the crimson plain, by the side of the Lost Sea of Korus, in the Valley of Dor, beneath the hurtling moons of Mars, speeding their meteoric way close above the bosom of the dying planet, I crept stealthily along the trail of a shadowy form that hugged the darker places with a persistency that proclaimed the sinister nature of its errand.

Action, description, and "sense of wonder buzz-words" (lost, hurtling, dying, stealthily) aplenty. Burroughs wastes no time in involving the reader. And perhaps there is a second reason for his popularity: his visual imagination. Long after one has forgotten the plots of the stories, long after John Carter and the beautiful Thuvia are all that remain of the participants in the sagas, one remembers the vivid detail of the landscape, the exotic, the rich, the startling colours, the wastelands of waving moss and lichen, the forests screeching with their populations of winged creatures "unlike any bird of earth". In *The Gods of Mars*, Carter and his green man colleague, Tars Tarkis, approach a sheer cliff, which must be surmounted; most writers would be content to try and dazzle you with scale. Not Burroughs:

The cliffs towered above me a good five thousand feet. The sun was not quite upon them and they loomed a dull yellow in their own shade...

... I was just on the point of motioning Tars Tarkis to follow me in that direction when the sun passed the cliff's zenith, and as the bright rays touched the dull surface it burst out into a million scintillant lights of burnished gold, of flaming red, of soft greens, and gleaming whites – a more gorgeous and inspiring spectacle human eye has never rested upon.

The face of the entire cliff was, as later inspection conclusively proved, so shot with veins and patches of solid gold as to present the appearance of a solid wall of that precious metal, except where it was broken by outcroppings of ruby, emerald, and diamond boulders...

No granite cliffs for Edgar Rice, but a failed prospector's wildest dream. And it is that descriptive excitement and engagement of the senses that makes Burroughs memorable, and has made of Barsoom a timeless, unforgettable realm of fantasy.

Others followed in the tradition of Burroughs, and later on Burroughs' Barsoom itself was parodied, used, exploited, much as Robert Howard's Hyborea was re-utilised by modern writers. Burroughs himself wrote a sequence of adventures set on Venus, but these were never as popular as his Barsoomian tales, or Tarzan of the Apes.

Of the later versions, Leigh Brackett is certainly the best, less an imitator, more a novelist in the same tradition (and a far, far better writer than Burroughs). Her sequence of novels set on verdant Mars is wonderful science fantasy, and the best is *The Sword of Rhiannon*. The Mars of this, and the other books, is again a Mars of the far distant past, which the hero, Matt Carse, visits after he has explored the *modern* ruins of the tomb of the ancient warlord Rhiannon. Possessed by Rhiannon's spirit, Carse is plunged back in time: "I have come into the past of Mars. All my life I have studied and dreamed of that past. Now I am in it. Matthew Carse, archaeologist, renegade, looter of tombs". Thus Brackett can contrast the dusty, dead sea bottoms of modern Mars, with the exotic, lustrous world of thousands of years before:

Before, the foxhole entrance to the Tomb of Rhiannon had been in a steep cliff-face. Now he stood on the grassy slope of a great hill. And there were rolling green hills and dark forest down there below him, where before had been only desert. Green hills, green wood and a bright river that ran down a gorge to what had been dead sea-bottom but was now – sea. And down on that far sunlit coast he saw the glitter of a white city. Jekkara, bright and strong between the verdant hills and the mighty ocean, that ocean that had not been seen upon Mars for nearly a million years.

Mars, as a place of rich plant and animal life,

was an established tradition by the 1930s, however one chose to explain the anomaly. And while pulp writers romped across their jungle landscapes, C. S. Lewis published the first of a trilogy of marvellous allegorical tales, *Out of the Silent Planet*, whose action takes place on the world known, to its gentle, wise inhabitants (the *hrossa*, the *eldil*, the *sorna*) as *Malacandra*. Mars. Elwin Ransom, a renowned philologist, is kidnapped by two men,

Preceding pages: *The skies above the great cities of the green martians on Barsoom are always dark with "naval vessels and public pleasure craft, flying long streamers of gay-coloured silks, and banners and flags of old and picturesque design". But the air, too, is a place of battle, as when the evil red martians attack a dead city, used by the green men. The "huge craft, long, low and grey-painted" pour fire down upon the city; but the fire is returned, and the great air-ships turn tail and run, all save one which is grounded and the occupants slaughtered.*

and by "means fantastic" the three of them travel to Malacandra, the kidnappers with ideas of plunder, Ransom as a hostage. The civilisation they find there is in harmony with itself, with nature, and Lewis uses literary conventions to contrast man's arrogance and turmoil with this Universal race of peace-loving creatures.

Like Burroughs, however, Lewis has a wonderful eye for detail and a rich sense of landscape. Ransom and his abductors land, on Malacandra, by a lake, in the purple twilight of a vast, flimsy forest:

> ...he turned his attention to the nearer shore beyond the shallows. The purple mass looked for a moment like a plump of organ pipes, then like a stack of rolls of cloth set up on end, then like a forest of gigantic umbrellas blown inside out. It was in faint motion.

Lewis portrays the idea of "alien" in a sequence of metaphors that leave one with an

Above: *"The dust of ancient hills whispered under the eternal wind. Phobos had set, and the stars were coldly brilliant. The lights of Jekkara and the great black blankness of the dead sea-bottom lay far behind and below them now." Matthew Carse climbs up the steeply-ascending gorge to the crumbling rock face, where the entrance to the tomb of Rhiannon lies, surmounted by an inscription in the ancient High Martian characters.*

eerie image of forty-foot high, quivering stems, topped by broad, translucent leaves, filtering the dim light between them. Malacandra is a place of strange perspectives, deep valleys, weird vegetation. The creatures that live there either inhabit the high land, the *harandra*, or the *handramit*, the deep, watered gorges that cut through the mountains, invisible to anyone looking from earth. As he journeys towards the Martian twilight, with several of the *hrossa*, Ransom observes how the deep gorges plunge into darkness early in the evening but, "the high country of the *harandra* still shone pale rose, remote and smooth and tranquil, like another and more spiritual world."

Another total contrast with the chaotic exoticism of Burroughs, and yet a Mars equally as memorable, if not more so, is the dying Mars that was described by Ray Bradbury in a whole series of stories known collectively as *The Martian Chronicles* (also published as *The Silver Locusts*). Where Burroughs' world was primitive natural selection, Bradbury's Mars is dry, silent, gentle, echoing. Bradbury's world appeals more, then, because it is a ghostly place, an echo of that realm of fantasy which, if imagination allows, it had been a million years before. The stories cannot help but appeal more, as well, since Bradbury - with different success according to different readers - has instilled into these tales of the gradual erosion of old Mars by new Earth, a set of moral fables, not conundrums, nor epistles, but elegant, elegiac songs, filled with poignancy, written with all the feel of a still, sad summer's evening. To read the stories is not to read a writer trying to impress with plot, or character,

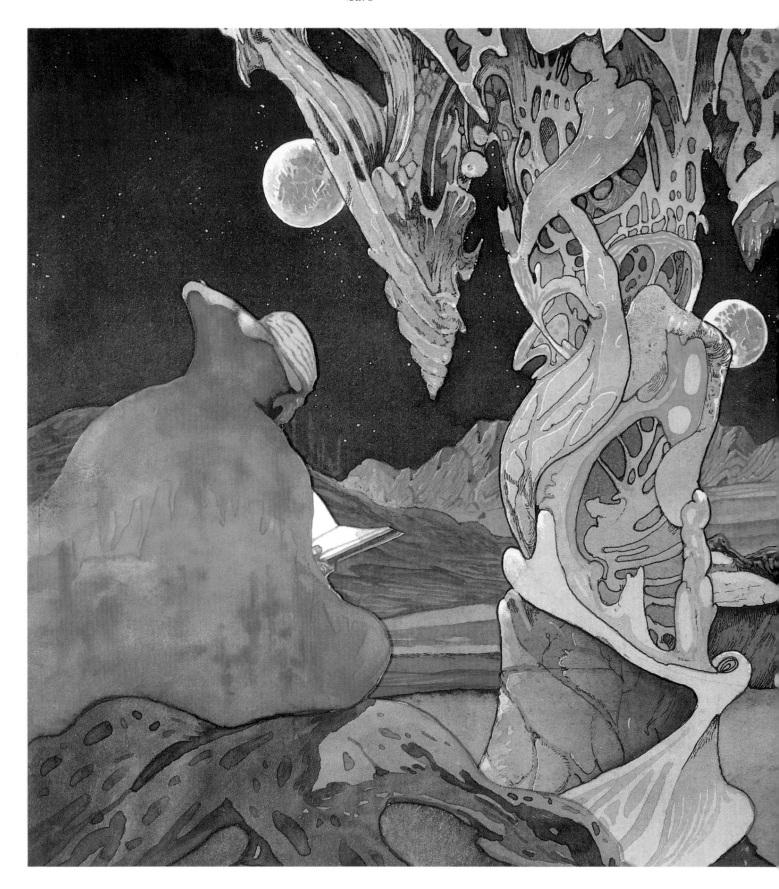

or sense of wonder, but to listen to the echo of a single man's sadness and confusion at the indifference of the world that encompasses him. The stories in *The Martian Chronicles* are more about you, the reader, than about Mars, the dying Martians, or the callous space-pilots and townies who invade them. If the style does not intrude between reader and prose – and alas, with some more literary conscious readers this is the case – they are fairy tales as effective and evocative as the work of Grimm or Andersen.

The whole ethos of *The Martian Chronicles* is pre-summarised in Bradbury's obscure, 1943 *Thrilling Wonder* story, "The Piper". Perhaps, having written "The Piper", Bradbury saw the potential of the theme, and re-designed his whole exploration of Mars. "The Piper" is about the last surviving Martian, Kerac, who is being shipped home from exile on a Jovian moon; his only skill is in the playing of a small set of pipes, and he is a renowned player. But when he arrives on Mars, he is deeply shocked to see the great sprawl of the Jovian cities that have obliterated the beautiful cities he remembers from childhood:

They left the rocket port, walked into the town, into narrow, alley-like streets, filled with the thick, fishy odour of Jovian food. Laughter echoed down crooked-spined thoroughfares. Glasses shattered. Now and then a gun snapped, propelling death, adding to the din of the alien city.

Preceding pages: *"They had a house of crystal pillars on the planet Mars by the edge of an empty sea, and every morning you would see Mrs K eating the golden fruits that grew from the crystal walls, or cleaning the house with handfuls of magnetic dust..."* *Mr and Mrs K's ancestors have occupied this house for ten centuries; like a flower it turns to follow the sun, and the view changes as the house revolves, sometimes a fossil sea, sometimes the deep canal where children still swim. Mr K spends his days reading the speaking books of the ancient Martians, which, as he brushes his hand over their metal pages, sing to him.*

Opposite: *In "Usher II" a man arrives on Mars to escape the censors of Moral Climates. He builds a funhouse like the House of Usher from Edgar Allan Poe's story, with mechanical creatures, such as the ape from the Rue Morgue, Trolls and Giants, harlequins, black cats and white queens. The house reverberates to the beat of a tell-tale heart, and the fairground dummies are far more deadly than they appear to be.*

Kerac is brutally beaten up and forced to demonstrate his musical skills. He impresses the Jovians, who are unused to artistic beauty, but who can faintly respond. What Kerac plays reflects his shock at the sight of his home world, obliterated and repopulated by the swaggering, coarse-mouthed Jovians:

Looking out over a dimly illuminated stretch of desert in one direction, the lifeless Martian city of Kam lay desolate. Kam's aged spires towered towards thin air, flinging out great symmetrically designed parkways and gardens like the unused pinions of a magnificent bird, for ever quiescent, no more to live, no more to fly.

But Kerac is aware that the mountainous regions of Mars are still inhabited by the Dark Race, shambling, semi-sentient beings, that are only awaiting the summons to rise and swarm through the invader's territory, obliterating it. But how to summon these creatures? Kerac finds the clue in the song of the birds, and he tricks the city's radio centre into recording his own piped version of that bird-song, and broadcasting it amplified across the public address system:

In five minutes the trails, the gullies, the hills and mountaintops were alive with a creeping, ever-changing line of amoeba-like figures that swarmed down in a huge tide. The tide crossed the river, slobbered along the highway, summoned by the music.

The Dark Race was not alone in the spell. Every Jovian in the city stood frozen, listening to the wondrous beauty of the music.

USHER II · 2003·

A "Marsquake" heralds the sudden arrival of the stampede of the Dark Race, and portends the destruction of the cities, the colonists, and the Piper who has summoned the Nemesis.

The *Chronicles* proper begin with the arrival of the first Earthmen, as seen by Mr and Mrs K, who "had a house of crystal pillars by the edge of an empty sea". Life is very still and tranquil for the Ks. Mr K spends most afternoons reading and staring out at the scenery: "The fossil sea was warm and motionless . . . and the little distant Martian bone town was all enclosed".

For a while, the Earthmen do not survive, but gradually they arrive in greater numbers, and their habitations grow, their influence spreads. Bradbury leads us through the change in a series of still-afternoon dreams. Do the stories connect or not? It is of no importance. As one reads, so the Martians have abruptly gone. The sense of timelessness on Mars remains, but now the perspective is human, humanity haunted by ghostly sounds on the dry winds. Time is at the centre of the *Martian Chronicles*.

There was a smell of Time in the air tonight. He smiled and turned the fancy in his mind. There was a thought. What did Time smell like? Like dust and clocks and people. And if you wondered what Time sounded like it sounded like water running in a dark cave and voices crying and dirt dropping down upon hollow box lids, and rain.

Time and ghosts, Bradbury plays with both, manipulating his prose with all the dexterity of a weaver. The Martian cities are white, like bones, like chess pieces, derelict, crystalline, reverberating and singing in the wind; human towns are stark, shanty towns, but soon they too become deserted, become Martian:

There was a little white silent town on the edge of the dead Martian sea. The town was empty. No-one moved in it. Lonely lights burned in the stores all day.

But man is not Martian, and the world, and its ghosts, begin to destroy him, making him homesick, making him "not-man". In "The Off Season", a failed hot-dog salesman, living with his wife at the junction of two empty highways across the planet's surface, is haunted by the apparition of a Martian, and runs from his house in a battered, very ancient "sand ship", a Martian vessel that had been used thousands of years before. As he runs, he takes out his despair and anger in the only way that he knows:

They were passing a little white chess city, and in his frustration, in his rage, he sent six bullets crashing among the crystal towers. The city dissolved in a shower of ancient glass and splintered quartz. It fell away like carved soap, shattered. It was no more.

The man has never seen a Martian, even though a few remain, hiding in the hills. He never *wants* to see a Martian. He's a frontiersman, with all the prejudices, fears and ignorances that go with the breed. So imagine his terror at what happens next:

The blue phantom ships loomed up behind them, drawing steadily apace. He did not seem them at first. He was only aware of a whistling and a high, windy screaming, as of steel on sand, and it was the sound of the sharp razor prows of the sand-ships preening the sea-bottoms, their red pennants, blue pennants unfurled. In the blue-light ships were blue-dark images, masked men, men with silvery faces, men with blue stars for eyes . . . Martian men.

Soon there is very little left, just empty towns, and houses that wake up in the morning and fall silent at night, but have no occupants. Man's indifference has destroyed the Martians, and then that indifference has turned back on itself, and man the invader has been destroyed as well. But not totally. The final image of *The Martian Chronicles* is of a gentler sort of man, showing his children the Martians that they have longed to see – he holds them up to the banks of a canal and they peer down into the rippling waters, from which the Martians gaze back at them...

Chapter Five

HYBOREA
The Realm of Conan

Illustrated by

David O'Connor

"'I saw the battlefield whereon I was born... I saw myself in a pantherskin loin-clout throwing my spear at the mountain beasts. I was a mercenary swordsman again, a hetman of the Kozaki *who dwell along the Zaporoska river, a corsair looting the coasts of Kush, a pirate of the Barachan Isles, a chief of the Himelian hillmen. All these things I've been, and of all these things I've dreamed; all the shapes that have been* I *passed like an endless procession, and their feet beat out a dirge in the sounding dust.'"*

Robert E. Howard
THE HOUR OF THE DRAGON

"As for Conan's eventual fate – frankly I can't predict it. In writing these yarns I've always felt less as creating them than as he told them to me. That's why they skip about so much, without following a regular order."

Thus, in a letter to his friend P. Schuyler Miller, Robert Ervin Howard hints at the genesis of his greatest, most memorable creation, the muscle-bound mercenary, the almost brainless "Fate-driven" adventurer, Conan of Cimmeria. "Conan simply stepped full-grown into my consciousness," Howard wrote about the character. He had stalked out of oblivion and "set" Howard to work, recording the saga of his adventures. Although Howard himself recognised how Conan was simply a combination of several men he had known – prize-fighters, gunmen, bootleggers and gamblers – he held to the romance of Conan's spiritual presence in his mind, thus explaining the non-chronological nature of the Conan stories: an old adventurer – now a king, but a brooding, haunted man – reminiscing on his past, would not be orderly in his narration of events.

Howard wrote only twenty-one Conan tales before his death at the age of thirty. Conan was not even Howard's favourite – he was far happier writing westerns – and he would arbitrarily assign his various creations – King Kull, or Solomon Kane, or Bran Mak Morn, or early Conan – to whatever plot took his fancy, depending upon which market was requiring the story, and how he felt at the time.

What, then, makes Conan so memorable? Might it be that Howard *was* drawing upon some supernatural source, stories narrated to him by the ghostly presence of the long dead adventurer? It is more likely that his comments to Miller reflect Howard's natural prolificness as a writer. He wrote fast, with amazing energy and great vitality, and under such circumstances a sort of "unconscious control" *does* take over a writer, and narration flows as if by magic. Howard's plots are now formulaic, but in his day, the twenties and early thirties, still could seem fresh. He wrote westerns, which were his main output during the last years of his life (and in which he has shown himself to

be a most witty and readable of writers); he was a prolific historical writer – and he could turn his hand to fantasy with the greatest of ease.

His fantasies are more often than not historical stories, made fantastic by name changes, settings that predate known history, and the presence of witches and wizards, and formless "gibbeths" summoned from the dark past. Often these weird inclusions in his stories serve no other function than to test the mighty strength of Conan in more bizarre ways: sword-fighting is one thing, but Conan must bludgeon his way through spells, curses, ghosts, giant snakes and monsters of loathesome appearance.

So do King Kull and the others. But Conan has been remembered; Conan was special. In recent years there has been a film made of this unlikely character; a Conan comic strip has been running for decades. Other writers, obsessed with Howard's characters, have completed unfinished tales, or written new adventures based upon them – and Conan has been the Howard character most subjected to this further exploration (and the only one who is in any way successful). The "new" stories are bloody, shallow, and often bad. And they are not Howard's Conan, try though they will.

What immediately strikes the new reader about Howard's original Conan, is the *restraint* of the stories. This may sound strange, as the generally held idea is that Conan is the most bloodthirsty of barbarians, and that each time he lifts his sword great gouts of blood and brains spurt from anything he has touched. Howard describes gore far less profusely than is imagined; he does, however, celebrate "power". Conan never stabs an adversary, he "hews limbs, heads and thews". Howard writes of characters and fights in ways that paint "power" pictures, rather than "gore" pictures, the image of the Ultimate Man, reducing life by nothing but his muscular ability. This is how he describes Conan:

> ...a tall man, mightily shouldered and deep of chest, with a massive corded neck and heavily muscled limbs. He was clad in silk and velvet, with the royal lions of Aquilonia worked in gold upon his rich jupon, and the

crown of Aquilonia shone on his square-cut black mane; but the great sword at his side seemed more natural to him than the regal accoutrements. His brow was low and broad, his eyes a volcanic blue that smouldered as if with some inner fire. His dark, scarred, almost sinister face was that of a fighting man...

Conan, indeed, is a primitive. He is one of the tribesmen whom Howard describes as living in the grey hills of the north, in Cimmeria. Repeatedly Howard reminds us that Conan is as "barbaric as any tribesman in the Cimmerian Hills", as the mercenary's patience is tested and tried and his teeth grind in fury and bloodlust. Even when he has become King of Aquilonia (a story well told in the only novel Howard wrote, *The Hour of the Dragon*) Conan's past betrays itself. His sense of honour is all his own, and is that of a tribesman. "I have no royal blood, I am a barbarian and the son of a blacksmith!" This in answer to a nobleman's insistence that – a battle having been lost – it would be the "part of majesty to yield with the dignity becoming one of royal blood". Conan refuses.

Conan's armour, as King of Aquilonia, consisted of black plate mail and visored salade. Over all there is a silk surcoat with the royal lion in gold upon the breast.

Conan is his own man, with a dignity measured in muscle power. He rejects tradition, weakness, he flaunts strength and self-centred aggression, and in this way speaks for the hero in us all, at odds with common sense. In his efforts to communicate this "strength", Howard's writing often goes hilariously right over the top: "The great muscles of his right arm swelled in anticipation of murderous blows".

Though on many occasions a sort of burning romance in Howard converts his overwriting into a prose that would not be amiss in any modern love story:

> He caught her up in his iron arms, crushed her slim, vibrant figure to him and kissed her fiercely on eyes, cheeks, throat and lips, until she lay panting in his embrace; gusty and tempestuous as a storm-wind, even his lovemaking was violent.

Sometimes he is downright awful: "Conan stood paralysed in the disruption of the faculties which demoralises anyone who is confronted by an impossible negation of sanity."

But one does not read Conan – nor, indeed Robert Howard – for style or literacy. One reads for the vitality and the image of his stories, the mind pictures of fabulous landscapes and towering, sinister ruins, of pageantry and the clamour of battles fought between opposed ranks of medieval knights.

For that is what the Conan stories really are: an admixture – not always successful – of historical landscape and culture, decked out with fantasy.

> The king, and his allies moved westward at the head of fifty thousand men – knights in shining armour with their pennons streaming above their helmets, pikemen in steel caps and brigandines, crossbowmen in

leather jerkins. They crossed the border, took a frontier castle and burned three mountain villages, and then, in the valley of the Valkia ... they met the hosts of Conan, king of Aquilonia – forty five thousand knights, archers and men at arms...

Howard repeatedly invokes the haunting images of long lost civilisations, forgotten cities, Ancient Wisdoms and the sense of a greater magic in days of old. His descriptions become very poignant because of this, and that poignancy, contrasted with the swirl and excitement of the action, creates an atmosphere about the Conan stories, and awareness of the greater world than that upon which the story is focussed. In "The Devil in Iron", for example, Conan must defeat a magician, resurrected after many thousands of years in his tomb on the mysterious island of Xapur, whose castle-like cliffs rise sheer from the ocean:

> It was uninhabited, all but forgotten, merely one among the myriad isles which dotted the great inland sea. Men called it Xapur, the Fortified, because of its ruins, remnants of some prehistoric kingdom, lost and forgotten before the conquering Hyborians had ridden southward. None knew who reared those stones, though dim legends lingered...

In "The Jewels of Gwahlur" Conan treks through jungle and surmounts the imposing cliffs that totally surround a lost valley, and the ruined city of Alkmeenon. How well Howard captures the timeless sense of ruin and decay of the crumbling domes and pinnacles of the once majestic stronghold, now haunted only by the ghosts of the dead past:

> All about him he saw signs of an ancient civilisation; marble fountains, voiceless and crumbling, stood in circles of slender trees whose patterns were too symmetrical to have been a chance of nature. Forest-growth and underbrush had invaded the evenly planned groves, but their outlines were still visible. Broad pavements ran away under the trees, broken, and with grass growing

Preceding pages: As Conan sails, in a war galley, along the river Styx, he sees the great black walls and towers of the city of Khemi rising against the Southern horizon; a city of the land of Stygia, now Egypt.

through the wide cracks ... Ahead of him, through the trees, the domes gleamed ...

But of course, Alkmeenon is far more dangerous than its deserted remains suggest, and magic and monsters are soon loosed upon Conan, who battles both to rob the city of treasure and prevent the death of a beautiful woman. The vile creatures and gruesome monsters that Conan tackles are strongly reminiscent of the shivering, quivering, croaking horrors that are so remarkably described in the work of H. P. Lovecraft. Perhaps Howard was influenced, perhaps not, though the two corresponded at length. At any rate, the language is the same, the descriptions of witches, weirds, and shambling nightmares from the "stygian night", or crawling from the "dark abyss of time" or the "black night of ages".

Howard is as enthusiastic in his portrayal of the women who inhabit Conan's world, and in every way that Conan is Super Man, Howard's women are slender examples of stereotyped femininity, such as Zenobia, who passes in front of a burning torch, whose glow "outlined her supple figure through the wisp of silk twisted about her loins, and shone vaguely on jewelled breast-plates. Her dark eyes gleamed in the shadows, her white limbs glistened softly, like alabaster. Her hair was a mass of dark foam..."

Girls are a major interest of Conan's. Girls and adventure, and gold, of course. What motivates Conan is self aggrandisement, and self satisfaction. He is ill at ease in politicking, and uncomfortable with success. It is the sense of *striving* for success that Conan enjoys, the sense of conquest. Howard leaves the reader in no doubt at all than Conan is not just monstrously strong, but also monstrously stupid. Intelligence flickers only dimly behind that "low broad forehead". When Conan speaks sense the sensation is disturbing. One is restless for him to be attacked by a gibbeth or wizard, or an army of fifty thousand, so that he can cut the clever stuff.

And yet, around this barbarian, worlds twist and turn, empires fall, armies collapse and great plots fall afoul of Fate. What emerges is the fascinating idea that greater forces than Man or Empires are playing Conan like a black knight in chess, racing him through the world and using him as a game piece in the destruction of Order. Motivated by greed, Conan appears to "blunder" into intrigues between states, and reduces all components to bloody dust. Fate smiles. Conan is entropy. He is an agent of Chaos in all but Howard's words. He helps keep the world fresh and changing, moving always forward. His stupidity immunises him to pain and assault; he has few feelings, save those that are animal:

> For an instant the future fate of kingdoms that hinged on this grey-clad barbarian hung in the balance. It was a small thing that tipped the scales – merely a shred of silk hanging on a bush ... He leaned to it, his nostrils expanding, his nerves quivering to a subtle stimulant.

Like a rogue tiger, Conan is certain and sound in his single direction, magnificent in his power and strength, terrifying to intelligent men who can recognise that his natural vigour is a great defence against their magic. Even nature recoils from him, as if perhaps most vividly shown in "A Witch is Born": Conan has been crucified. As he strains to tear himself from the twelve-inch iron nails, the vultures swoop on him, pecking at his eyes. Conan bides his time, and as one of the huge beasts flies at his head, Conan strains rapidly forward and clamps his teeth around the vulture's neck, hanging on grimly, "the muscles starting out in lumps on his jaws. And the scavenger's neck-bones crunched between those powerful teeth. With a spasmodic flutter the bird hung limp". Not surprisingly, the other vultures don't hang about.

The Conan stories are epic fantasy in the oldest tradition. He adventures in lost, labyrinthine cities, on remote island, or within hidden valleys. He encounters re-animated sorcerers and demons, shambling monsters, evil princesses. He fights giant apes and serpents, he heroically saves beautiful women. But mostly, the Conan stories draw upon the tradition of war, the splendid engagement of

armoured armies, from the lands of the Cossacks, the Persian Empire, the Celts, and of course, the mediaeval battlefields of Roland and Henry the Second.

And this, perhaps, is the simple reason for Conan's popularity: Howard *built* the world-scape across which Conan moves, working out the prehistoric landscape in great detail. Conan's homeland, Cimmeria, is but one part of the world of Hyborea, and within Hyborea the reader finds many things to recognise, such as Picts and Nordics, who loosely conform to the historical peoples of those names, but who are immensely more powerful and widespread in Conan's time.

Howard wrote a long essay on the subject of Conan's landscape. Called *The Hyborian Age*, it was published in 1936, although Howard had prepared it before beginning his cycle of Conan stories, that is, before 1932. The essay is merely an account of how the "lost epoch" of the Hyborian Age developed from just after the sinking of Atlantis, right through to its final form as we now know it: which is to say, our own European continent. It's a pseudo-history that must have given the author a great deal of pleasure to work out, and its supposition that *long before* recorded history begins there existed a complex civilisation, of knights and magic, upon our own European landscape, is very appealing.

Howard's Hyborea was a continent raised higher above sea level than the Europe of today, so that the continental shelf around our coasts are land, and the whole of the British Isles are "highlands" occupied by ferocious Picts. The ancient countries and cities that were Hyborea are long forgotten, but some of them remain as myths and folk memories (said Howard) and thus we find countries called Afgulistan, Iranistan, Corinthia and mountain ranges termed the Himelians, beyond which lie the golden lands where "Devi" rules.

Howard prepared a map of Hyborea, which

Preceding pages: The mountains of Hyborea are remote and dangerous places. Fog-shrouded gorges, beast-infested caves, and other worldly magic makes Conan's journey truly hazardous.

was more clearly drawn out by John Mayers for the 1977 Berkeley edition of the Conan novel, *The Hour of the Dragon*. (Three volumes of Conan stories were produced by Berkeley, edited by Karl Wagner. They are identical with the original published versions from *Weird Tales* magazine, and include the re-instatement of much offensive material relating to Blacks and Racial Purity previously edited out). The map shows the land of Cimmeria as covering what is now Northern England, Denmark and Southern Norway. The bulk of Scandinavia was the Kingdom of Asgard. What we know of as Germany was, in the Hyborian Age, Nemedia, whilst Western Russia was known as Brythunia. France lay below the Kingdom of Aquilonia. West of Cimmeria, which is to say, west of the British Isles, were the Pictish Wastes (now buried below the sea). The Mediterranean Ocean was also land – Argos in the west, and Shem in the east, and from Shemites, driven further east during invasions by Nordic races, came the Arabs, Israelites and Kushites... Howard hardly missed a trick in this elaborate construction of fantasy. Egypt consisted, then, of a series of small kingdoms: Stygia, Keshan, Punt and – interestingly enough – Zembabwei.

The pseudo history is an account of wars: between the Aesir and Vanir, which were pure-blooded, and the swarthy races of Picts and Cimmerians; between the Hyrkanians and Aquilonians, the Shemites and Bossonians. It is an account of failed annexations, barbarian hordes, mercenary atrocities, raiders, reavers, and armies on the march. It is an account of lands cracking and the seas rising...

The whole essay is reminiscent – a sort of "pre-echo" – of the account of the history of Middle Earth, as compiled by J. R. R. Tolkien at the end of *Lord of the Rings*. It is a sign of the power of the imagination at work, and one wonders what realms of great fantasy Howard would have explored had he lived.

Robert Howard died at the age of 30, in Cross Plains, Texas, the town where he had lived all of his life with his parents. He died in the driver's seat of his car, shot in the head with a .38 calibre Colt automatic, which he had borrowed; a self-inflicted wound. On his type-writer he had written only:

All fled – all done, so lift me on the pyre;
The feast is over and the lamps expire.

This last, poignant piece of verse concluded a writing career that had produced over 160 published stories, numerous works of prose, and a voluminous correspondence between Howard and various of his peers in the world of pulp literature. If he died with any regrets it is likely that they were that he had never met his friend H. P. Lovecraft, indeed had never travelled much beyond Cross Plains. It is recorded that Howard was immensely frus-trated at not being able to meet Lovecraft when the writer visited New Orleans in 1932. Howard was broke at the time, and Lovecraft on a tight financial schedule. It was a fact of life for those who earned a living from the pulps, that one month a cheque would elevate the writer to solvency, and the next, a magazine's demise, or a story rejection, could threaten further months of poverty.

The reason for Howard's suicide is well known. He was devoted to his mother, fixated upon her to an unusual – a psychiatrist would say abnormal – degree. When she developed cancer, Howard spent a small fortune, and much of his time, trying to obtain appropriate medical treatment for her. When she finally went into a coma, Howard was calm and quite collected; he established clearly that the coma was "terminal" and then carried through his intention to suicide with ease and, it would seem, without compunction. Indeed, Howard's father, a medical man, had long been aware of his son's death wish, his fascination with suicide and the nobility of death.

In a way, then, both Howard's life and death were dictated by that same fatality and destiny that governed characters in his fantasy worlds. There would be a time in life in which to achieve a certain amount, and then it would be time to go; the forces of Order would protect him for 30 years, but Chaos would have its way at a moment marked out by the Gods.

One can certainly regret the loss of the writer that Robert Howard might well have become;

and it is easy to rue the awfulness of so much that he left behind, and the feeling of incompleteness of so much else. But Howard nonetheless has left behind a legacy of great spirit, stories on an epic scale, a hint of past worlds that can excite even the most cynical reader's sense of wonder.

Howard was a true storyteller, relegating "life and character" to a very low second place. Adventure, exoticism, and expression of Man as ideal, Man using natural wits and animal cunning, rather than elegant philosophy and rationalisation, these were the stuff of Howard, and he did it remarkably well.

He always believed that a lot of him – an alter ego, perhaps – was present in his main characters. His friends, also, could see a great deal of Howard in his stories. There is no doubt that the author invested his tales with that particular intensity, and energy, which comes from deep, almost passionate involvement with the writing. Howard would have loved to have been many of his characters; they seem to reflect different aspects of Howard's dreamed-of self-image: strong, sturdy, indomitable, self-contained wanderers, adventurers, men with hearts of iron, wills of steel, committed to nothing and no-one – and yet with compassion.

Howard was none of these things, it would seem, save compassionate. He weight-trained and body-built, in his adult years, to approximate to his physical ideal, and was thus a sturdy, broad-shouldered, immensely powerful man when he died. And yet in photographs he looks soft, chubby, a man haunted by regret that he *was* the way he was. As for being a wanderer, a man sufficient unto himself ... Alas, he was dependent on another not just for happiness, but for life itself. And when that other was no longer there, nor could Howard be.

And so he roamed the world of time and space in his mind. He read voraciously about exotic places, and then filled out the many gaps with imagination and invention. His real worlds are no more realistic than his fantasy worlds. Arabia or Hyborea, Africa or Lemuria, London or Alkmeenon, all existed in one place only, in one realm of fantasy only: the mind of the writer.

Chapter Six

ATLANTIS

Illustrated by

Chris Foss

"We came in sight of the peak of the sacred mountain, with its share of eternal fires which stand behind the city... The wind was adverse, and no sail could be spread, but under oars alone we made a pretty pace. The sides of the sacred mountain grew longer, and presently the peaks of the pyramids in the city, the towers of the higher buildings, began to show themselves as though they floated upon the gleaming water. It was twenty years since I had seen Atlantis last, and my heart glowed with the thought of treading again upon her paving-stones.

"The splendid city grew out of the sea as we approached, and to every throb of the oars, the shores leaped nearer. I saw the temple where I had been initiated to the small mysteries; and then...I made out the house where a father and mother had reared me, and my eyes became dim as memories rose."

C. J. Cutliffe Hyne
THE LOST CONTINENT

What images are brought to mind by the name "Atlantis"? Perhaps a bright and beautiful land, lying far off across the glimmering blue Atlantic, its cities raising bright spires to the sky, its streets a bustle of civilisation and contentment, a culture far in advance of our own. Perhaps the name conjures a vision of sea-ruins, a vast island rising slowly from the ocean once every few hundred years: through its weed-strewn streets, among the salt-caked stone ruins, walk a few mariners who have stumbled upon the lost world by chance. They slip on the wet cobbles, force through rusted doors into empty, silent halls and chambers, and eventually run back to their ship as the island trembles beneath their feet and slowly subsides below the waves. Maybe Atlantis brings to mind a totally submerged civilisation, a great city, protected from the ocean's pressures and cold by a vast dome; at night, lights can sometimes be glimpsed through the depths.

However Atlantis is seen by the imagining mind, all visions are right – and none. Atlantis is one of the earliest realms of fantasy, and its nature, its purpose, and its mythology changes with the ages, adjusts to suit the temperament, beliefs and needs of the culture which is contemplating it. Perhaps there was a real, geographical location which was destroyed by the elements and gave the impetus to the story: the destruction of Thera, perhaps, in the fourteenth century BC, or the disappearance of the city-state of Tartessos from the south-western shores of Spain in the fifth century BC. But Atlantis has always meant, "The place beyond the western reaches where there is a lesson to be learned about civilisation". Utopia, perhaps, or how Utopia can fail through arrogance. However storytellers have used Atlantis, the fantasy realm of their tale was directly related to their real realm.

The Atlantis story begins before Plato, although it is first known from his writings. Plato, an Athenian, lived from 427 BC until 347 BC. He was a philosopher, who used a standard technique of his day for getting his philosophy across: plays, in the forms of dialogues between famous men. In his plays *Timaios* and *Kritias*, Socrates chats with friends, and one tells the story of Atlantis; and the tale which he tells has been obtained from an Egyptian priest by the Greek philosopher Solon, nearly three hundred years before.

After the Creation, the gods shared up the world between them, and the goddess of wisdom, Athena, acquired Greece; she established the first Athenian state, ruled by a military caste, of great courage and virtuousness. The sea god, Poseidon, had received Atlantis for his share of the world, and he mated with a human female and produced ten sons, each of whom became king of an Atlantean state. All this occurred (said Plato) nine thousand years before that modern Athens. For centuries the Atlanteans were as virtuous as the Athenians, but a streak of corruption and greed soon brought the Atlanteans to the East, to make war of gain against the Greeks.

The gods, it seems, punished Atlantis. The brave Athenian army defeated the marauding Atlanteans, but suffered themselves in the cataclysm that Zeus – presumably – launched upon the world. Athens was engulfed by a huge earthquake, the Straits of Gibralter were closed by mud, and to the far west, the continent of Atlantis, "larger by far than Africa and Asia Minor combined", sank below the waves.

Plato's version of an earlier legend was clearly allegorical, and designed to discuss, compare and contrast the perfect state, as he had outlined in his *Republic*, with an apparently perfect state where human weakness could still prevail and cause social breakdown.

This allegorical interpretation prevailed for centuries, until, during the later Roman Empire, writers – for example Proklos – began to attach reality to the tale, taking Atlantis seriously, and setting the scene for the "belief" in the lost continent that would develop later.

Atlantis slipped from general awareness until the middle of the second millennium, when the great explorations began, sailors and adventurers from Italy, Spain, England and Holland striking out for unknown worlds. Islands, new continents, new lands, all tend to feature strongly on maps of that time. The places, usually non-existent, are often interpretable as misplaced sitings of the Azores, say, or the coastline of Newfoundland. Atlantis

is often "marked", a fancy that one would have thought dangerous to subsequent generations of mariners.

At this time, Sir Francis Bacon wrote *The New Atlantis*, and helped sow the seeds of the later romantic Atlantis revival. Bacon's book was an allegorical and religious tract, featuring Atlanteans who had fled to the south seas when their continent had been devastated by flood. Bacon drew upon Thomas More's *Utopia*, and thus the image of Atlantis was re-established as a place of great advancement, devastated by the seas consuming it.

Interest was further generated by Abbé Charles-Etienne Brasseur de Bourbourg in the 1860s. Brasseur discovered a completely erroneous "pictogram alphabet" of the old Mayan language, which had been compiled three hundred years before by a Spanish priest called Landa. Nonsense though this alphabet was, Brasseur translated one of the few remaining tracts of Mayan writing and discovered references to "...the upheaved earth ... the place engulfed beneath the floods ... the basin of water..." Later, the correct translation of what appeared, to Brasseur, to be an account of the destruction of Atlantis, proved to be a tract about astrology!

Nevertheless, an American, called Ignatius Donnelly, drew upon what had gone before – however incorrect – and began the cult of *Atlantism*, citing similarities in life style between American Indians and Europeans (marriage, religious beliefs) as evidence for both sides of the Atlantic having been "influenced" by a greater, cradle-culture living between. Atlantis was the place from which all things civilised had come!

By Donnelly's time, no-one seriously expected to see Atlantis on the surface of the ocean, although the legend remained that, at times, Atlantis *did* rise from the sea. Many works of fiction drew upon this idea, even as Jules Verne was having the sunken, dead remains of Atlantis explored by Captain Nemo, and other writers were constructing the vast dome that kept water out, and the sterile Atlantean culture intact below the ocean's waves. Nemo, of course, in recent films has been shown to have "conquered" this enclosed land below the sea, so that modern victims of shipwreck find themselves on the set of *two* story fantasies – (first) the land of Atlantis ruled over, (secondly) by Verne's inventive submariner. Atlantis is so strong a myth that it remains good for screen mileage, if no longer an attractive prospect in literature.

Nowadays, Atlantis features in fiction in its "long, lost" form. If the ruins remain below the seas, there was a time, before history began, when Atlantis was a real land...

Atlantis was the setting for Robert E. Howard's first series of heroic fantasy. Featuring *King Kull* it is in many ways the prototype for Conan. Howard's Atlantis is backward and primitive, not at all the cultured, advanced civilisation from which all knowledge had once come. Kull is a savage from the stone age, who quits Atlantis for the mainland the Thuria, where he fights as a mercenary, becomes King of Valuria, and encounters much that is magic along the way.

Later, Howard banished Atlantis below the waves, and the stage was set for Hyborea to emerge upon the European continent.

A more recent addition to the body of literature taking mythical Atlantis as its base is Jane Gaskell's elegant trilogy of novels concerning the minor Goddess, Cija of Atlantis. The books, *The Serpent*, *The Dragon* and *Atlan*, tell of the invasion of Atlantis by an army from the north, of its General's uneasy reign upon the throne of Atlan, and his eventual demise when Ancient Atlan unleashes her own forces. Gaskell's Atlantis is protected from the eyes of man because her scientists have surrounded the continent with an impenetrable vacuum, drawing in the air from over the sea for a mile around it. But the invasion force follows the heroine of the tales, Cija, through a secret tunnel of glassy substance, which enables them to cross below the airless sea.

The mythic association of a continent that has been submerged is so strong that even Tolkien has such a lost land, referred to in *The Lord of the Rings*, and described in *The Silmarillion*. It is the vanished continent of Númenor, destroyed as punishment for its people seeking immortality; this idea links exactly with Plato. The story of the loss of

Númenor is one of the most vivid of the fabulous sequence of fragments that form *The Silmarillion*, and is described in the legend of *Akallabêth*:

> In that time the fleets of the Númenóreans darkened the sea upon the west of the land, and they were like an archipelago of a thousand isles; their masts were as a forest upon the mountains, and their sails like a brooding cloud; and their banners were golden and black.

This is a Númenórean invasion fleet, come to wreak havoc upon the land. But the "father" God Ilúvatar will not permit such evil, and destroys the fleet of the Númenóreans, and also the armies of the men they faced:

> And a great chasm opened in the sea between Númenor and the Deathless lands, and the waters flowed down into it, and the noise and smoke of the cataracts went up to heaven, and the world was shaken. And all the fleets of the Númenóreans were drawn down into the abyss, and they were drowned and swallowed up forever.

Ilúvator goes further, however, and destroys the land itself:

> Then suddenly fire burst from the Meneltarma, and there came a mighty wind and tumult of the earth, and the sky reeled and the hills slid, and Númenor went down into the sea, with all its children and its wives and its maidens and its ladies proud; and all its gardens and its halls and its towers, its wisdom and its lore: they vanished forever.

In an interesting postcript to this tale, Tolkien writes of how the lost lands are thereafter referred to as "Mar-nu-Falmar, that was whelmed in the waves, of Akallabêth the Downfallen, Atalantë in the Eldarin tongue". And so the legend of Atlantis gets a new interpretation.

But if one work of fiction can be said to have done justice to the legend of Atlantis, it is C.

J. Cutcliffe Hyne's *The Lost Continent*, published in 1900. It's a novel in the best "lost world" tradition for the central action occurs at a great time in the past, and is recorded in a manuscript discovered in the modern day. The manuscript itself is an account of Atlantis at the time of the great civilisation of Egypt. Indeed, Hyne's Atlantis is a continent with a semi-Egyptian culture sprawling on its shores, but a remote and monster-infested heartland. The city where the Empress resides stands below the sacred mountain, on which eternal fires burn; great pyramids rise above the temples and houses; galleys bob and speed through the enclosed harbours, mostly manned by slaves from Europe, who are regarded as little better than animals.

The story tells of the attendance of Deucalion upon the Empress Phorenice, of his love for a banished girl, and his own banishment to that monster-infested jungle in the heart of the continent, and of the final catastrophe that frees him, a passenger aboard an unlikely vessel: an Ark, "rudderless, oarless, and machineless. The inside was dark, and full of an ancient smell, and crowded with groanings and noise."

The end is dramatically described, an ideal conclusion to this chapter on Atlantis:

> Far out on the distant coast [the sea] surged against the rocks in enormous rolls of surf; and up the great estuary, at the head of which the city of Atlantis stands, it gushed in successive waves of enormous height which never returned. Already the lower lands were blotted out beneath the tumultuous waters, the harbour walls were drowned out of sight. [Soon] the plains and the level lands were foaming lakes. The great city of Atlantis had vanished eternally. The mountains alone kept their heads above the flood, and spewed out rocks and steam, and boiling stone, or burst when the waters reached them, and created great whirlpools of surging sea, and twisted trees, and bubbling mud.
>
> And then ... a vast hurricane of wind must have come on next so as to leave no piece of the desolation incomplete.

Chapter Seven

MELNIBONE
Moorcock's Chaos and the Eternal Champion

Illustrated by

Mark Harrison

"He saw Imrryr as it had been many centuries ago. Imrryr, the same city he had known before he led the raid on it and caused its destruction. The same, yet with a different, brighter appearance as if it were newly-built. As well, the colours of the surrounding countryside were richer, the sun darker orange, the sky deep blue and sultry. Since then, he realised, the very tints of the world had faded with the planet's ageing...

"People and beasts moved in the shining streets; tall, eldritch Melnibonéans, men and women walking with grace, like proud tigers; hard-faced slaves with hopeless, stoic eyes, long-legged horses of a type now extinct, small mastodons drawing gaudy cars. Clearly on the breeze came the mysterious scents of the place, the muted sounds of activity – all hushed, for the Melnibonéans hated noise as much as they loved harmony. Heavy silk banners flapped from the scintillating towers of bluestone, jade, ivory, crystal and polished red granite. And Elric moved in his sleep and ached to be there amongst his own ancestors, the golden folk who had dominated the old world."

Michael Moorcock
STORMBRINGER

For a while, in the late 1960s, it seemed (in Britain, at least) that the realm of fantasy had become a one-man show. That one man was Michael Moorcock, and his slim volumes of "Sword and Sorcery" proliferated on the bookshelves as if self-reproducing. Over six years he produced innumerable books dealing with the heroic figures and fantastic landscapes of times long in the past, or far in the post-holocaust future, all linked through what he termed the "Multiverse". If those volumes peter out, both in the intensity of their imagination, and the energy of their prose, for the most part they are haunting and absorbing tales of adventure, brought to richly visual life by the fertility of the author's imagination, and by the exquisite descriptions of the bizarre and mythic landscapes and beings that inhabited that creative well.

Moorcock was born in 1939, and became editor of *Tarzan Adventures* at the age of 18. In 1957, too, he published the first of his sword and sorcery stories, tales which were later gathered together in *Sojan*. In recent years he has become acclaimed as one of Britains most original and imaginative of novelists, but in the early days, at least, he was a devotee of Edgar Rice Burroughs and Robert E. Howard, and his first work followed in their footsteps.

Nevertheless, even in those days Moorcock clearly saw both the weakness and the potential of the fantasy form to which he was to apply himself over the next few years. Influenced by Mervyn Peake in part, and outdoing Lovecraft for "horribleness" without sinking to Lovecraft's lamentable depths of purple prose, Michael Moorcock was more concerned with the "adult themes below the action", with combining what he terms the "picaresque theme – the quest theme" of traditional narrative with the exploration of

Preceding page: *In the remote, post-apocalyptic future of Moorcock's* Runestaff *series the Camargue region of France, where giant flamingos and horned horses run wild across the marshes, has become the feudalist state of Count Brass, who has his power base at Castle Brass. Count Brass is never seen without a carapace of brass armour.*

Opposite: *"Nikorn's palace was a fortress, bleak and unlovely. It was surrounded by a deep moat of dark, stagnant water, built into, rather than onto, the rock... The rock was porous in places, and slimy water ran down the walls."*

the "haunted palaces of the mind" that pre-occupied the writers of Gothic novels, and the more contemporary Mervyn Peake himself.

In the books dealing with Elric of Melniboné, at least, Moorcock was seriously concerned with creating both mythic landscapes and character interplay, and with seeding the whole with a meaning that – as in all good fiction – needed not to be stated for its presence to be felt. He was contemptuous of fantasy writers who regarded themselves as writers of "adult fairy stories". Most were not, he argued. Most merely wrote fairy stories for adults who still wanted to *read* fairy stories. "The writer who merely recaptures the dream-worlds of childhood without adding to this what his adult mind has learned is an inadequate artist, if nothing else."

There is nothing artistically inadequate about Moorcock's fantasies. They are richly textured, often savage, tightly plotted adventures, bursting with ideas and characters. The perception is adult, even when a vein of self-parody creeps into the later books.

Two concepts quickly evolved as the sequence of fantasy novels unwound: that of the "Multiverse", and that of the Eternal Champion.

The Multiverse is Moorcock's way of linking different times, different cultures, different realities. He explains that multiple alternative realities co-exist in a single Universe, all of them able to interact destructively at the hands of the Lords of Chaos. Thus is linked the pre-dawn civilisation of Melniboné, from which Elric Womanslayer emerged (one of the four human facets of the Eternal Champion) with the post-holocaust world of Dorian Hawkmoon, and with the exotic, decaying landscapes of Prince Corum and Erekosë.

To date, in the sequence, the Eternal Champion has been represented by these four heroic figures:

Four tall, doom-haunted swordsmen, each of a strikingly different cast of features, yet all bearing a certain stamp which marked them as being a like kind.

Each in their own way different, each is a part of the same mythic figure, destined to fall always between the opposed forces of Law and Chaos. This is the basic conflict in most of Moorcock's work, and it reaches beyond his fantasies and into his most memorable books, those featuring Jerry Cornelius. The Eternal Champion. in whatever guise, rides the chaos landscapes (those places where entropy strives to increase) struggling to resolve the conflict between the unsentimental, self-seeking, almost cruel forces of both Law and Chaos. Whatever the nature of the minds behind those tendencies, neither side is a friend to Man, both sides seeking to use any member of the human race they can.

Elric of Melniboné is one such who has been used. An albino, a warrior prince outcast from his own land, he carries his sentient, life-seeking sword *Stormbringer* as he journeys (in the stories concerning him) across the most imaginative of Moorcock's fantasy landscapes, seeking revenge for the killing of his cousin, and lover, the beautiful Cymoril.

At his hip rests his runesword of black iron – the feared *Stormbringer*, forged by ancient and alien sorcery when Melniboné was young. In many ways, the sword is the hero of the Elric stories, for it possesses an intelligence more evil than Chaos itself; it has already destroyed its twinned weapon *Mournblade*, and only its symbiotic need for Elric himself gives it any form of controlled existence. The sword, forged by Gods before the world has evolved the human form, is an evil and terrible object:

Preceding pages: Imrryr, the Dreaming City, the most beautiful of the cities of Melniboné. In The Stealer of Souls *Elric leads his war-galleys against the city. But at its height, the great city is a place of gentle towers, brilliant art, and a wide, still harbour, protected from the ocean by cliffs through which pass labyrinthine water-ways, complex enough to snare the unwary and unwelcome sailor.*

Opposite: Order finally triumphs at the end of Stormbringer. *Elric blows the Horn of Fate to "herald in the new night of the Earth"; the huge outline of a hand holding a balance appears in the sky and then Elric's sword,* Stormbringer, *leaps from its scabbard and slays him, a last savage act.*

A doomed and dreadful symbiosis existed between man and sword – they needed each other. The man without the sword would become a cripple, lacking sight and energy – the sword without the man could not drink the blood and the souls it needed for its existence. They rode together, sword and man, and none could tell which was master.

It remains ambiguous as to when, in time as we know it, Melniboné flourished; the far past, the far future? *Time is an agony of Now*, declares the introduction to *The Stealer of Souls*, and in the concept of the Multiverse, past and future interact through the present. What is clear, though, is that the Bright Empire of Melniboné flourished for ten thousand years, ruling the world. But ravaged by the formless terror called Time, Melniboné at last fell and newer nations succeeded her: Ilmiora, Sheegoth, Maidahk, S'aaleem. Then history began: India, China, Egypt, Assyria, Persia, Greece and Rome – all came after Melniboné, although none lasted ten thousand years.

Melniboné fell because it was attacked by powers greater than men, shaken by the casting of frightful runes. Elric is one of the few of Melniboné's scattered sons who remember the ancestral powers, the magic that allows him to call upon dark forces as he battles against sorcerers, evil Queens, armies of the dead, bizarre and grotesque creatures which inhabit the ruined, decaying landscape.

In stark contrast to the timeless world where Elric quests, the world of Dorian Hawkmoon – whose adventures make the *Runestaff* and the *Chronicles of Count Brass* – is Southern France of the future, specifically Kamarg:

It had taken all these five years to restore the lands of the Kamarg, to repopulate its marshes with the giant scarlet flamingos,

the wild bulls and the horned great horses which had once teemed here, before the coming of the Dark Empire's bestial armies.

Across this futuristic European landscape, Dorian Hawkmoon quests to discover the secret of the Runestaff, battling the evil Count Brass, and laying siege to his tall-towered, white-walled castle.

Erekosë, who was the first form of the Eternal Champion which Moorcock explored, is a 20th century man – John Daker – snatched by mystic forces from his tomb to a time far distant when the Eldren are threatening humanity with extinction. With his sword *Kanajana* he becomes Vengeance Bringer, "humanity's scythe to sweep this way and that and cut the Eldren down as weeds".

And even further in the future than Hawkmoon's Kamarg (although, with the concept of the Multiverse, we may be in the remote past again) the landscapes in which Corum, Prince in the Scarlet Robe, adventures are exotic in the extreme, and occasionally show Moorcock's imagination working in overdrive:

In those days there were oceans of light and cities in the skies and wild flying beasts of bronze. There were herds of crimson cattle that roared and were taller than castles. There were shrill, viridian things that haunted bleak rivers.

The time of Corum is a time of Gods, manifesting themselves upon our world in all their aspects; a time of giants who walk on water, of mindless sprites and misshapen creatures which can be summoned by an ill-considered thought, but driven away only on pain of some fearful sacrifice. Moorcock is still unbeatable when it comes to writing an enthralling tale, but by the time of the Corum books, despite such occasional flourishes, his energy and inspiration is flagging, and an almost offhand style replaces the starkly striking visual quality of earlier description.

The city of Imrryr:

Built to follow the shape of the ground, the city had an organic appearance, with winding lanes mounting like a chord of

Above: *The Camp of Chaos, from Stormbringer. The Ships of Hell move both on sea and on land, sailing slowly through the fires and palanquins of the gathered hordes of chaos creatures. The Ships are immense – like galleons, but a hundred times as tall. They tower over a landscape that boils and heaves. A strange and eerie light envelops the ships and the landscape, through which shamble the living dead who crew the vessels.*

music up to the crest of the hill where stood the castle, tall and proud and many-spired, the final, crowning masterpiece of the ancient forgotten artist who had built it. But there was no life-sound emanating from Imrryr the Beautiful, only a sense of soporific desolation.

Or the decaying fortress of Nikorn:

...a fortress, bleak and unlovely. It was surrounded by a deep moat of dark, stagnant water. It stood high above the surrounding forest, built *into* rather than *on to* the rock. Much of it had been carved out of the living stone. It was sprawling and rambling and covered a large area, surrounded by natural buttresses. The rock was porous in places, and slimy water ran down the walls of the lower parts, spreading through dark moss.

There is more than a touch of Peake's influence in such description, but Moorcock is such an individualist that his books can never be seen as anything but his own, and he takes both received and interior vision, and fashions them remarkably. Upon the ruined landscapes, and within the corridors and towers of his cities and fortresses, characters with names like Tanglebones, Moonglum, Count Brass, King Urish the Seven Fingered (with his axe, *Hackmeat*) swagger and creep, each truly memorable. And creatures, too: Wind Giants, Mist Giants, leathery-winged apes, dragons, and chaos creatures of every imaginable demean; and creatures from the dark, like Arioch, the amorphous, soul and bone consuming demon who is Elric's familiar, or Quolnargn, a life-sucking hell-beast, that feeds on adults but "occasionally, as an appetizer, enjoys the morsels, the sweetmeats as it were, of the innocent life-force which it sucks from children."

Michael Moorcock himself now dismisses the whole sequence of heroic fantasies as hackwork; at least, that sequence which follows on from his best known creation, Elric of Melniboné. They were written, we are told, to obtain funds for his struggling, and excellent magazine, *New Worlds Speculative Fiction* (which was not surviving on an Arts Council Grant of £300 a month, and which was in total chaos in its offices in Ladbroke Grove). In any event, the magazine continued to struggle in all but the excellence of its content, and Moorcock developed a body of fantasy works that could have benefitted, towards the end, from a more considered, and less cynical approach.

In the early days, however, he clearly took the work more seriously, seeing possibilities in even the sword and sorcery form that he felt were abused in pure science fiction (which he considered to be a sub-genre of fantasy). He wrote that the good sword and sorcery story should have something of the function of a moving belt, perhaps, carrying the reader with it. "The dream-worlds of these stories are worlds to which writer and reader initially escape. They leave *everything* behind. The dream-landscapes and structures [the less limited writer discovers as he creates a story] will soon be utilised for his own artistic purpose, if he has any. He will apply his skill and understanding to making these worlds relevant to our own situation."

Even at that time (1963) his disillusionment with that quite valid sentiment is apparent, the failure of motive in the face of a readership not sophisticated enough to read more deeply. Investing the stories with a certain relevance to the reader's own society is what Moorcock tried to do with the Elric tales – evidently without much success since the less escapist themes he tried to carry within the sword and sorcery vehicle managed to elude a great many readers. "I shall have to try again with a fresh or altered vehicle".

That "fresh or altered vehicle", of course, was Jerry Cornelius, who in various guises (Jherek Carnelian, Jhary-a-Conel etc.) increasingly featured in Moorcock's work after 1965. Cornelius, in one sense, inhabits the same multiverse as do Elric and the other facets of the Eternal Champion. Like Elric, Cornelius is constantly torn between Law and Chaos, Order and Entropy. But to begin with, at least, Cornelius' landscape was the contemporary setting of London, in particular the area around Ladbroke Grove where Moorcock lived. But the London of Jerry Cornelius varies, is manipulated by – and manipulates – the character and his associates. The imagery is often of decay and ruin, visually haunting sequences that perhaps derive substantially from Moorcock's own vivid recollections of the bombing of London during the war. Cornelius is a sort of '60s culture anti-hero, through whose witty, often savage perspective the decay of urban London is observed, and the struggle for survival documented.

The man who began his literary career enjoying the influences of Howard and Burroughs, and particularly of Peake, by the mid-sixties was an influence himself. That influence has not declined, and nor has the originality of Moorcock's voice and vision. Writers imitate him; but he is inimitable. When he took over the editorship of *New Worlds Science Fiction* in 1964, he rapidly brought to the magazine – until then a staid and traditional sf outlet – a heightened awareness of human values, and a bold experimentalism with style and literary texture. The magazine was never commercially popular, and despite the enthusiastic editorship of Moorcock, Arts Council Grants, and private contributions from a few of the authors, *New Worlds* folded in 1971 (although it continued as an anthology).

Moorcock's best work has been written *since* New Worlds, an intermixture of sf, fantasy and history, which draws particularly on Edwardian society. He won the 1977 *Guardian* fiction prize for *The Condition of Muzak*.

Nearly thirty years after his first units of "heroic fantasy", Moorcock remains a writer of the times; his whole career is like the multiverse that his characters inhabit.

Chapter Eight

EARTHSEA

Illustrated by

Stephen Bradbury

Monochrome by Mark Harrison

"For four generations of men all ships had set their course to keep far from the shores of Pendor Island. No mage had ever come to do combat with the dragon there, for the island was on no travelled sea-road, and its lords had been pirates, slave-takers, war-makers, hated by all that dwelt in the southwest parts of Earthsea. For this reason none had sought to revenge the Lord of Pendor, after the dragon came suddenly out of the west upon him and his men where they sat feasting in the tower, and smothered them with the flames of his mouth, and drove all the townsfolk screaming into the sea. Unavenged, Pendor had been left to the dragon, with all its bones, and towers, and jewels stolen from long-dead princes of the coasts of Paln and Hosk."

Ursula Le Guin
A WIZARD OF EARTHSEA

Ursula Le Guin's world of Earthsea makes its first appearance in two short stories – "The Word of Unbinding" and "The Rule of Names" – both of which were first published in 1964 and reprinted in her collection *The Wind's Twelve Quarters*. Le Guin has said that she "didn't know much about the place at first", and apart from the fact that both stories are fantasies and set on islands there is little to connect them. "The Word of Unbinding" even introduces trolls, which are not present in the world of the novels. The dragon which appears in "The Rule of Names" is heard from again, but as Le Guin puts it, his history is "somewhat obscure". When the stories were written she had no clear mental map of Earthsea.

Earthsea, then, is not a world planned in detail like the fantasy realms of Tolkien or Donaldson. "I am not an engineer, but an explorer. I discovered Earthsea," Le Guin has written, and she did not embark on a full-scale exploration until invited to write a children's novel in 1967. Thinking about the islands, and

Preceding pages: *For generations, sailors had set their course to keep far away from Great Pendor. Lords of Pendor had been hated pirates and slavers, so few mourned when a dragon came suddenly out of the west, and destroyed the Lord and drove the townspeople into the sea. Now Pendor was abandoned to the dragon and its offspring, and its hoard of jewels.*

Opposite: *Beneath the Place of the Tombs of Atuan lay an immense labyrinth, and directly below the Tombstones themselves was a great vaulted cavern, the Undertomb. For generations no priestess had seen the Undertomb, because lights of any kind were Forbidden. Then Ged came in search of the missing half of the Ring of Erreth-Akbe, lighting the way with his wizard's staff. "It was jewelled with crystals and ornamented with pinnacles and filigrees of white limestone where the waters under earth had worked, eons since: immense, with glittering roof and walls, sparkling, delicate, intricate, a palace of diamonds."*

the magic that could be worked there, she came to wonder about wizards. What were they like before they became the elderly, wise, white-bearded figures usually portrayed in fantasy novels? Where did they learn to be wizards? From this idea grew the novel *A Wizard of Earthsea*, and from the novel grew the Earthsea trilogy.

Earthsea is an archipelago of innumerable islands measuring some 1500 miles from north to south and the same from west to east. The largest of the islands, Havnor, is about the size of Great Britain, but most of them are much smaller. There is a hint on the map of a larger area of land in the north, but for all practical purposes Earthsea is a world without continental landmasses.

The Earthsea books differ from the others discussed in this volume because they were first published – and indeed are still largely published – as children's books. Yet they are widely read and enjoyed by adults, and anyone who comes to Earthsea looking for simplification in ideas and emotions will be disappointed. They are books which have youthful protagonists, for when they were first published fantasy had still to establish itself as an adult genre, Tolkien's success notwithstanding, whereas it had an honourable and continuing tradition in children's literature. Therefore such writers as Le Guin and Alan Garner were most conveniently published as children's writers, but that does not imply any inferiority in their work as compared to that of adult writers.

Good children's books have, of course, always enjoyed an appeal to readers of all ages. This is because they do not talk down; they recognise that children deserve to be provided with books written in lucid and comprehensible prose, but dealing with real people and real problems. *A Wizard of Earthsea* deals with coming of age; *The Tombs of Atuan*, second book of the trilogy, to some extent deals with a similar theme from a female point of view, and is concerned with sex, in its broad sense; *The Farthest Shore* is about death, hardly a childish subject.

A Wizard of Earthsea opens on the island of Gont, a place famous for producing wizards.

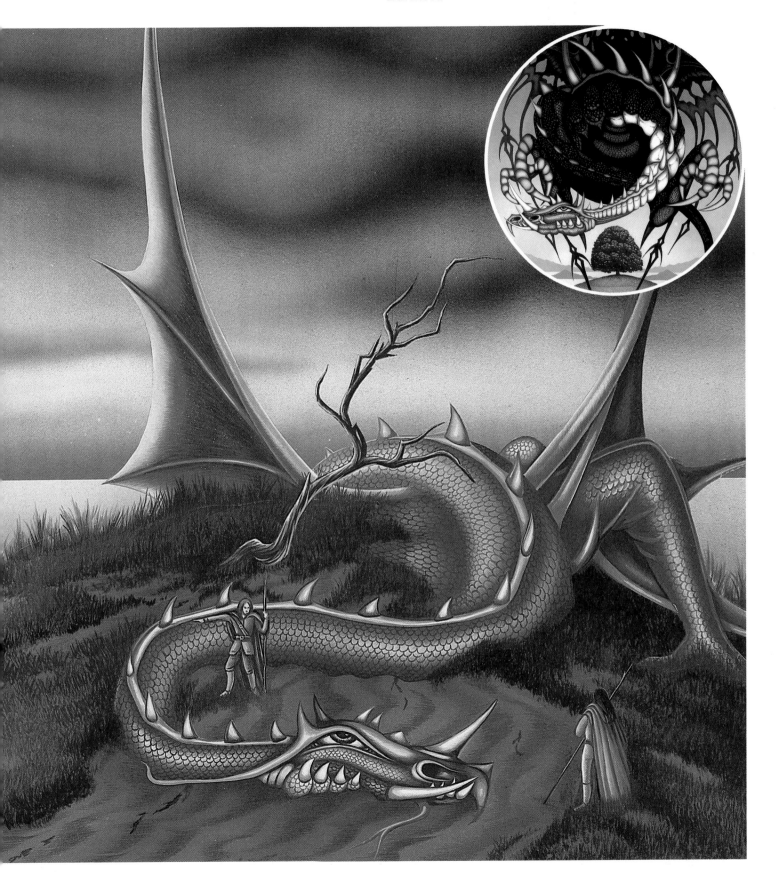

Preceding pages: *"This was the westernmost cape of all the lands, the End of Earth." On a beach, a beach of ivory-coloured sand was something like a hut, or shelter. At first sight it looked like driftwood, but closer examination showed it to be built out of huge bones – the bones of long-dead dragons. It had a doorway, whose lintel was an immense thigh bone. On the lintel stood a human skull. Before it lies Orm Embar, the mightiest dragon of all."*

Below: *"Down the far side of the hill of being lies the land of the dead. The sky is black and filled with small, cold stars unlike those which shine on the land of the living. The dead are numerous, but their land is very large so they appeared few in number. They were not frightening or loathesome; but quiet, devoid of emotion, devoid of all feeling, as dark and empty inside as their dark realm."* It is here that Ged and Arren must travel to restore the balance between the two worlds.

The young boy Duny finds in himself an aptitude for wizardry, a power which depends on knowing the secret true names of people and creatures and objects (a person's true name is not the name by which they are called). Soon Duny uses his powers to save his village from invading marauders, which brings him to the notice of a local wizard, Ogion the Silent. From Ogion he learns his true name, Ged; from the people of Gont he acquires the name by which he is outwardly known, Sparrowhawk.

In time Ged is sent to the School for Wizards on the island of Roke, where he studies the lesser art of the sorcerers: "windbringing, weatherworking, finding and binding, and the arts of spellsmiths and spellwrights, tellers, chanters, healalls and herbalists". He also begins to learn the basis of more powerful magics, an area in which he has already unwisely dabbled, being at this time a proud and headstrong boy. The magic used in Earthsea is complex stuff, and wizards must be trained in it as rigorously as scientists are

trained in our world. Much simple magic is simply clever illusion. The natural equilibrium of the world is not easy to alter, even by magical means. Only powerful mages may work such magic, and it is draining of their energy. Magic is not a gimmick, it is part of a philosophy: in this case of harmony and balance in nature, which relates (like the philosophy of much of Le Guin's sf) to Taoism.

But Ged, being impatient, tries to go too far too soon, and in attempting to impress his fellow pupils by summoning a spirit from the dead he also releases something else, "something like a clot of black shadow, quick and hideous ... that clung to Ged, tearing at his flesh. It was like a black beast, the size of a young child, though it seemed to swell and shrink; and it had no head or face, only the four taloned paws with which it gripped and tore." What has been released is, in fact, the dark side of Ged's character, the destructive force which lurks within us all. For the remainder of the novel either this shadow is in pursuit of Ged, or,

later, he is chasing it, because the two must reunite to be complete; whether Ged is destroyed or made whole depends on which of them is stronger; and if Ged is to be stronger he must outgrow the destructive immaturities of his childhood.

As a young wizard Ged travels to the isle of Low Torning, which is under threat from the dragons which have settled on nearby Pendor. Still pursued by his shadow, he feels he is endangering all around him, and therefore volunteers to go to Pendor and attempt to defeat the dragons, so that his obligation to the people of Low Torning will be ended. Pendor was once a prosperous and inhabited isle, but the dragons have destroyed or driven away the populace, and have settled amid the ruins of the town. Ged approaches in his small sailboat, powered by the magewind which he can summon, and defeats and destroys several of the smaller dragons. But it is the patriarch – the Old One – which he must somehow defeat. He calls to it where it lies hidden in the ruins of

the town, but only when it moves does he discover that it was in plain sight all the time:

Then Ged was aware that the highest tower slowly changed its shape, bulging out on one side as if it grew an arm. He feared dragon-magic, for old dragons are very powerful and guileful in a sorcery like and unlike the sorcery of men: but a moment more and he saw this was no trick of the dragon, but of his own eyes. What he had taken for a part of the tower was the shoulder of the Dragon of Pendor as he uncurled his bulk and lifted himself slowly up.

Whenever dragons enter a scene in the Earthsea books they always dominate it: along with the careful logic of magic they are the memorable creations of the trilogy. They are not merely huge and powerful animals, to be slain by a powerful hero; they are ancient, wise, devious, and endlessly fascinating. If they cannot overcome by simple physical power they can lure the unwary to doom by their command of language. One does not relax in the presence of a dragon. They have literary antecedents, most obviously Smaug in Tolkien's *The Hobbit*. But where Smaug was cunning and clever there was never any doubt of his intention, which was to preserve and increase his hoard and destroy anyone who might threaten it. The dragons in the Earthsea books are more complex beings. They must be restrained, but they may also in the right circumstances be powerful allies, as indeed Ged makes use of them in *The Farthest Shore*. Le Guin excels throughout at conveying both their ancient wisdom and the grandeur of their physical presence. Here, from the end of *The Farthest Shore*, is another encounter:

Its head, the colour of iron, stained as with red rust at nostril and eye socket and jowl, hung facing him, almost over him. The talons sank deep into the soft wet sand on the edge of the stream. The folded wings were partly invisible, like sails, but the length of the dark body was lost in the fog.

It did not move. It might have been crouching there for hours, or for years, or for centuries. It was carven of iron, shaped from rock – but the eyes, the eyes he had dared not look into, the eyes like oil coiling on water, like yellow smoke behind glass, the opaque, profound, and yellow eyes watched Arren.

This is fine writing, without the excess of adjectives which mars too much fantasy when the authors strive for effect. Here everything is calm, measured, almost quiet – but the image is evoked with great vividness. Le Guin is widely acclaimed as one of the major stylists in modern sf and fantasy, and from examples like this it is easy to see why.

The contrast between *A Wizard of Earthsea* and *The Tombs of Atuan* could hardly be greater. It is almost as if Le Guin has gone out of her way to avoid charges of cashing in on a success, by writing a sequel which is as far removed as possible from "Further Adventures of Ged". Indeed, Ged does not appear until halfway through the book, and while *Wizard* is a wide-ranging tale, carried by the magewind to far corners of Earthsea, *Tombs* is narrow, claustrophobic, confined. Much of it takes place underground, in a labyrinth.

The viewpoint character is a girl, Tenar, who at the age of five is selected to become a priestess of the Tombs on the remote island of Atuan. It is a dark and unfulfilling life, and the main story is of the bond which grown between her and Ged (who is initially her captive), and her escape with him from Atuan and into the outside world. Ged has come to Atuan to find the missing part of the ring of Erreth-Akbe, the other half of which he discovered (though he did not know it at the time) in *A Wizard of Earthsea*. The ring is engraved with powerful runes, but when it was broken one of them was lost – the rune which can be used to bring peace to Earthsea. There are obvious similarities here to *The Lord of the Rings*, but whereas the powerful ring in Tolkien's epic can be used only for evil, and corrupts anyone who attempts to harness its power, the ring of Erreth-Akbe can be used for good.

In *The Farthest Shore* the canvas is, once again, a broad one; indeed, there are more memorable descriptive passages here than in either of the previous books. But the subject, as we have said, is death, which on the face of it could not be more sombre, particularly in what is ostensibly a children's book. But Le Guin does not present death as something to fear; indeed, the threat to Earthsea in *The Farthest Shore* comes from a mage who has discovered a way of achieving a kind of immortality. But it is a meaningless kind of existence, because it is the fact of death which gives meaning to life. As Ged puts it: "No births; no new lives. No children. Only what is mortal bears life... Only in death is there rebirth. The balance is not a stillness. It is a movement – an eternal becoming."

In science fiction it has become something of a cliche that immortality brings with it boredom and sterility (both literal and metaphorical); in a fantasy novel Le Guin is able to dramatise the idea with great power. The dubious achievement of the magician Cob destroys the balance of which Ged speaks, and all Earthsea is threatened. "There is a hole in the world," Ged says, "and the light is running out of it." Ged must journey with the young prince Arren to the farthest shore – the land of death itself – to restore the balance; but ultimately he (who is now Archmage of Earthsea) can achieve this final victory only at the cost of his own powers.

En route he travels to some fascinating corners of Earthsea. Out beyond the archipelago, for example, Ged and Arren meet the Children of the Open Sea, who spend their lives on a flotilla of rafts, coming to land only once a year but otherwise following the migrations of whales. In an article on the background of the Earthsea trilogy, Le Guin mentions that these raft people were a central part of a story she tried to write between "The Rule of Names" and *A Wizard of Earthsea*, but it did not gel and was left incomplete. Not until she wrote *The Farthest Shore* did she discover the place in the story where they fitted.

But the strangest journey they must make comes at the end, when they pass through a gateway into the land of the dead:

It seemed that they walked down that hillslope for a long way, but perhaps it was a short way; for there was no passing of time there, where no wind blew and the stars did not move. They came then into the streets of one of the cities that are there, and Arren saw the houses with windows that are never lit, and in certain doorways standing, with quiet faces and empty hands, the dead.

This is no conventional hell; the essence of Le Guin's land of the dead is that it is still, grey, free of emotion – lifeless, in other words.

Among all the fantasists discussed in this volume Le Guin is the one who most clearly dramatises moral and ethical questions in her work. She has lucidly criticised Tolkien's detractors for looking for ideological messages which simply are not there: "Those who fault Tokien on the Problem of Evil are usually those who have an *answer* to the Problem of Evil – which he did not. What kind of answer, after all, is it to drop a magic ring into an imaginary volcano?" Of course it is no kind of answer at all, and yet fantasy novels do deal in archetypes, dramatising on a large canvas the battle of good and evil, order and chaos. Authors like Tolkien and Donaldson and Moorcock may be oversimplifying, in terms of the real world, and their solutions may not be transferable to the real world; still, they resonate in the reader's mind.

Le Guin, however, focuses more closely on the individuals; each of the Earthsea novels shows a character – Ged, Tenar, Arren – confronted with difficult choices, and emerging into adulthood. The threat which Ged and Arren must oppose in *The Farthest Shore* may, if unchecked, devour Earthsea, but it is not something unloosed by a mad magician out to dominate the world; rather, it is the by product of someone's natural, but immature wish to avoid the inevitability of death. Because all the books deal with coming-of-age, the discovery of maturity, they are suited to an adolescent readership; but because this is a transition into adulthood they are equally accessible and enjoyable to adults who have made that passage. The Earthsea trilogy is full of wonders – the many and varied islands, the carefully-worked-out magic and lore, the ancient and immense dragons – but it is the least escapist of fantasies.

Chapter Nine

THE LAND
of Thomas Covenant

Illustrated by

Mark Harrison

"At once, an immense panorama sprang into view below him, attacked his sight like a bludgeon of exhilaration and horror. He was on a stone platform four thousand feet or more above the earth. Birds glided and wheeled under his perch. The air was as clean and clear as crystal, and through it the great sweep of the landscape seemed immeasureably huge, so that his eyes ached with trying to see it all. Hills stretched away directly under him; plains unrolled toward the horizon on both sides; a river angled silver in the sunlight out of the hills on his left. All was luminous with Spring, as if it had just been born in that morning's dew.
"'Bloody hell!'"

Stephen R. Donaldson
LORD FOUL'S BANE

The most popular of Tolkien's successors is without doubt Stephen R. Donaldson. His first novel, *Lord Foul's Bane*, appeared in 1977, and it was followed in quick succession by the other books which make up "The Chronicles of Thomas Covenant the Unbeliever" – *The Illearth War* and *The Power That Preserves*. The books were not, at first, spectacular bestsellers, but they soon began to build an audience, and to sell very well indeed. As this book is written the last volume of the "Second Chronicles", *White Gold Wielder*, has yet to appear, but the first two novels, *The Wounded Land* and *The One Tree*, have climbed high on the bestseller lists on both sides of the Atlantic. From this standpoint, Donaldson (still in his early thirties) is a far more successful writer than Tolkien was in his lifetime.

Yet what is now such a success story could not have looked more unpromising a few years ago. Donaldson left graduate school late in 1971, having been awarded an MA but failing to complete a doctorate, and began writing full-time in January 1972. At the time he had not published or sold anything, but he was determined to be a writer and, he says, "I had learned enough about myself by then to know that I was never going to make it as a writer on a part-time basis. I didn't have the kind of mind that could produce good fiction part-time. I needed to be able to concentrate one hundred per cent." When the opportunity to write full-time arose he had no hesitation in giving up his academic career and jumping at it.

The first few months were spent working on a spy novel (which remains unpublished). Then, in the summer of 1972, the ideas for the Thomas Covenant trilogy came together and he started work. It was his first attempt at fantasy (though he had been writing copiously, and planning to be a writer, since 1964), and he acknowledged that the complete imaginative freedom of fantasy was what he needed to be successful. "If I know too much about something from direct personal experience, my imagination freezes up and I find that I write very dull prose. So I don't draw characters from life. I hardly ever draw situations from my own experience. In fact, my editor can go through a

manuscript and infallibly pick out all the passages where I did research, and he always forces me to rewrite them. He says, Look, forget the research, *make it up*... Before I tried any fantasy I kept writing very realistic mainstream types of fiction and kept forcing it on my friends to read. The reaction was always very negative in one way or another. Just in terms of being able to strike some interest in some of my friends my writing was *very* unsuccessful until I got into fantasy. I was writing about things that I knew about. They always tell you that in creative writing classes: write about something that you're familiar with. Well, I was doing that and the results were not *alive* on the page. I wasn't using my imagination in the way it was made to be used; I didn't know myself well enough to know what I needed to trigger my own creative juices."

For a long time, though, it did not look as if Donaldson's fantasy would prove any more successful. When he had finished a draft of *Lord Foul's Bane* he began to submit it to American publishers who published fiction. It was rejected by all of them, including the magazines which serialised fantasy and science fiction. He had, in all, 47 rejections – more, even, than the number totted up by another "unpublishable" book, Richard Adams's *Watership Down*. (As noted in the first chapter, *The Silmarillion*, too, was rejected when first submitted. It is not uncommon for books which fail to fit publishers' current conception of the "market" to be rejected widely, but Donaldson's experience, like Adams's, shows that an author who has faith in his or her work can go on to prove the publishers spectacularly wrong.)

While this weary and dispiriting process continued he had time to rewrite *Lord Foul's Bane*, to write and rewrite the other two volumes of the trilogy, and to rewrite *Lord Foul's Bane* yet again. By the time he ran out of publishers the trilogy was finished and Donaldson was in despair. "There's no way, looking back, that I can put into words the extremity of my emotional state at the time. I was in a terrible state. I'd done the best work that I knew how to do in the field that I loved the most, and as far as I knew every

professional there was, was convinced that my work was inadequate. By then I had really put myself in the position where it was writing or nothing with my life ... and it seemed fairly obvious at that point that it was not going to be writing."

Donaldson decided to start trying the book on British publishers, and sent away for a directory to work through. While he was waiting he could not bear to have the typescript, all 2400 pages of it, sitting on his desk, so he sent it again to Ballantine Books, one of the publishers who had previously turned it down. What he did not know was that they had a new fantasy editor, in the person of Lester Del Rey. He jumped at the book, and by the time Donaldson's directory of British publishers arrived it was no longer needed. The rest is history. As Donaldson puts it, "Since then I have had just the opposite kind of experience. The books have sold phenomenally well, I have been phenomenally well-treated, and I have had a phenomenal amount of respect in quarters that surprised me. It's really very hard to think that we're talking about the same books here. I mean, they *are* the same books!"

It would be absurd to deny that Donaldson's trilogy echoes, in many ways, *The Lord of the Rings*. Its fantasy world is threatened by a twisted and evil Lord whose dominion will destroy all that is good and beautiful in it. The hero must, in the end, journey to the very heart of that Lord's domain to do battle with him. One can readily draw up lists of equivalents. (Lord Foul = Sauron; Foul's Creche = Barad-Dur; the Ravers = the Nazgul; the ur-viles = the orcs; Mhoram = Gandalf, etc etc.) But for all

Opposite: *The old songs said that the High Lord Kevin stood here and surveyed the whole of the Land and its people, so that the place was named Kevin's Watch. A narrow splinter of stone, five hundred feet in length, it pointed up from the side of a cliff at a steep angle, like a finger pointed at the sky. Stairs, steep as a ladder, were cut into its upper surface. It was from here that Covenant first saw the Land to which he had been summoned.*

Following pages: Coercri, *or the Grieve, was the ancient home of the Giants, and it was a city built on a truly giant scale. A human figure was dwarfed by it, like a doll inside a cathedral. At the only quay still intact, lay the Giantship,* Starfare's Gem. *Here Covenant, with his White Gold magic, made a* Ceamora, *a healing fire, to free the spirits of Giants slain by a Raver, the agent of Lord Foul.*

these formal similarities – some of which are direct influences, some of which arise more from the fact that Donaldson and Tolkien are working within a similar epic tradition whose elements are fairly formalised – it is more interesting to look at the differences, which in the end make Donaldson's a quite dissimilar work.

The most crucial of these arise from the character of Thomas Covenant, and the way in which his adventure is framed. He is alone among the characters in the epic fantasies discussed in this book in being a character from our world. At first a contented and successful author, his life is shattered when he learns that he has contracted leprosy. The progress of the disease is arrested – as can readily be done if it is detected early – but he loses two fingers, and finds when he returns to society that fear of the disease makes him an outcast. His wife leaves him; his friends and neighbours shun him. He becomes deeply embittered. Then, walking about town, he meets a strange beggar, a blind man leaning on a staff, who tells him:

"Take back the ring. Be true. You need not fail."

Subsequently he falls in front of a police car, and in the semi-conscious daze which follows is somehow transported to another world, the Land. The Land is a place of remarkable beauty and serenity; a world in which magic resides in the very trees and rocks. Here, Covenant finds that his disfigurement marks him as a great returned hero, the legendary Berek Halfhand, while his white-gold wedding ring is an object of great magical power. There

is even a mud which appears to cure his disease. Everything, apart from the threat of Lord Foul, is idyllic in the Land:

> Covenant stopped to gaze, entranced, down the length of the valley. It was no more than fifty yards long, and at its far end the stream turned left again and filed away between two sheer walls. In this tiny pocket in the vastness of the mountain, removed from the overwhelming landscapes below Kevin's Watch, the earth was comfortably green and sunny, and the air was both fresh and warm – pine-aromatic, redolent with springtime. As he breathed the atmosphere of the place, Covenant felt his chest ache with a familiar grief at his own sickness.

But Covenant is too alienated and embittered to accept his apparent good fortune. At an early stage he betrays the trust of the people who have accepted him by raping the girl who first found him, Lena. And he is unable to believe in the Land itself.

This is unusual. It is common enough in fantasy and in early sf (such as Burrough's Mars books) for a character to be transported from our world to another, by dream, by astral travel, or by more inexplicable means. Once they are there, however, they soon cease worrying about the mechanism and get down full-heartedly to their adventures. Covenant, however, knows his Freud. The theme of the story is common too – a character with some flaw is involved in a series of adventures, in the course of which this flaw is worked out. It is a central theme of fantasy. Where Covenant differs is that he suspects it is a fantasy being played out in his subconscious, that Lord Foul is a symbol, and that the Land is something he has dreamed up to translate into acceptable

Preceding pages: *"The trees were generally taller and broader than their southern relatives; abundant and prodigal* aliantha *sometimes covered whole hillsides with viridian; the rises and vales luxuriated in deep aromatic grass. The Andelanian Hills carried a purer impression of health than anything else he had experienced."*

terms the ideas which his bitter conscious self cannot cope with. In other words Covenant is aware of all the points that a critic might make in discussing a novel of this kind, which gives the work an added layer of sophistication.

Moreover, in the first trilogy Donaldson offers no disproof of Covenant's hypothesis. In the second volume he meets another character, Hile Troy, who appears also to come from his Earth. But when, back in our world, he tries to check up on Troy's existence he gets nowhere. True, there are people, such as the beggar or a girl in a nightclub who greets Covenant as "Berek", who seem to have a connection with the Land, but it is vague enough to permit alternative explanations. Only in the second trilogy, when Covenant has a companion, the woman doctor Linden Avery, does the doubt seem to disappear. Donaldson also makes this uncertainty central to the plot of the trilogy. Because Covenant does not believe in the Land he cannot properly fulfil the role which destiny has in store for him there. And because he is partly of our world he twice is transported back to it at crucial moments – and finds, when he returns to the Land, that years have passed there during his (subjectively) short absences.

Covenant, too, is an unlikely character: an embittered leper as the hero of a fantasy trilogy? He becomes more likely, however, in the context of Donaldson's own background. His father was an orthopaedic surgeon and worked for twenty-one years in India (where Donaldson was brought up), where he spent a considerable amount of time treating patients at the local leprosarium. To Donaldson, then, "the idea of a leper was always a very *normal* one. We encountered none of the hideous dimensions that the illness can under some circumstances take on; on the other hand, for the last ten years I was in India our gardener was a leper, and a perfectly normal fellow he was too." Back in the USA he became conscious that for many people the horror of the disease was still alive (and indeed it was possible for it to progress further without treatment, because it was not a disease doctors expected to encounter – unlike in India – and therefore it was not usually diagnosed quickly). Thus it was natural when conceiving of an alienated character that Donaldson should seize upon leprosy to symbolise him. The character of Linden Avery in the "Second Chronicles" is also emotionally disturbed, and indeed Donaldson says that the characters in most of his unpublished fiction and other published stories are similar, an obsession he ascribes in part to guilt at not having followed in his father's footsteps as a doctor.

It is impossible to read far in Donaldson's work without becoming aware that he uses a great many unusual words. It is not uncommon in fantasy to find authors using odd sentence constructions and some antiquated vocabulary to establish a feeling of distance and strangeness, but Donaldson takes this further than any other modern writer except Gene Wolfe. (However, Wolfe confines his arcane words and coinages to nouns – the names of social groups, and military ranks, and animals and so forth, which are different in his world than in ours; he describes them in formal but conventional prose. Donaldson throws in adjectives of extremely obscure origin, and comes up with very odd metaphors and similes). He admits that "I do get carried away in matters of language and sometimes overdo the business of using unfamiliar or arcane words. Nevertheless, there are many good reasons to do so, one of which is that every writer who cares about the English language has a certain responsibility to the language itself to keep it alive and flexible and current. Another is that in a fantasy world particularly, some of these words have flavours that you can't get from day-to-day usage. A word like 'caducity' or 'tabid' or 'atrabilious' has a different kind of feeling from the modern equivalent, and these feelings are appropriate in certain settings. I don't do this kind of thing in an effort to confuse my readers!" While this is fair and valid, it must be admitted that Donaldson does sometimes carry matters to extremes, using obscure words where common ones would do just as well, and occasionally coming up with something wholly incomprehensible: "They were featureless and telic, like lambent gangrene." It is anyone's guess what that is supposed to convey.

Following pages: A river of seething molten rock, Hotash Slay guarded the entrance to Foul's Creche. It spouted lava and brimstone, but was weirdly silent. Beyond lay the Creche itself – two slender towers, hundreds of feet high, with between them the single entrance. Most of Foul's demesne lay underground – his breeding dens, storehouses, barracks and throne.

Donaldson originally had no intention of following the first trilogy with further Thomas Covenant books: "I have a horror of sequels. Other people's sequels almost always disappoint me terribly. I thought there could be nothing stupider than to try and write a sequel." But Donaldson's editor had other ideas, and in an effort to prod him into action kept putting forward his own ideas for possible sequels, knowing what the eventual effect would be. "His suggestions were all *terrible*. They just made me cringe. One of them was so bad that before I could stop myself I was saying no, I can't do that, what I really ought to do is – and before I knew it I had practically a whole story laid out in my head, and furthermore it implied a further story beyond *that*. So I was looking at two more trilogies after I had thought the first was self-contained."

Comment on the "Second Chronicles" should properly await its completion, but it must be said that in the first volume, *The Wounded Land*, Donaldson's portrayal of the Land sickened and poisoned by the "sunbane" created by Lord Foul is one of his most effective pieces of writing to date, while the journey to the Land of Faerie and the episode of the Sandhold in *The One Tree* show his invention to be as fertile as ever. Donaldson's popularity continues to grow, and it seems that in a few years time – when the Second, and it would seem from his remarks, the Third, Chronicles of Thomas Covenant are complete, he will have created the most massive and detailed fantasy world of all.

(Note: All quotations attributed to Stephen Donaldson in this chapter are taken from an unpublished interview with the author conducted by Malcolm Edwards.)

Chapter Ten

URTH
The Ancient Future and the Book of the New Sun

Illustrated by

Michael Johnson

"I have heard those who dig for their livelihood say there is no land anywhere in which they can trench without turning up shards of the past. No matter where the spade turns the soil, it uncovers broken pavements and corroding metal; and scholars write that the kind of sand that the artists call polychrome (because flecks of every colour are mixed with its whiteness) is actually not sand at all, but the glass of the past, now pounded to powder by aeons of tumbling in clamorous sea."

Gene Wolfe
THE SHADOW OF THE TORTURER

The realms of fantasy are usually worlds set either somewhere in our distant and forgotten past, or are worlds which exist somewhere *other* than our own – such as Tolkien's Middle Earth, which shares many aspects of our myths and legends, but is not our world. There is a third option available to the writer, however, though it is one which is only rarely used: the distant future.

Arthur C. Clarke once composed an aphorism – subsequently dubbed "Clarke's Third Law" – which states that any sufficiently advanced technology is indistinguishable from magic. It follows from this that a story set far enough ahead in our technological future may become indistinguishable from fantasy; its magicians may be manipulating advanced scientific techniques, but to us it will look as though they are performing magic.

·The first significant story to take us into the unimaginably distant future was William Hope Hodgson's *The Night Land*, first published in 1912. Here, the narrator makes a dream journey millions of years into the future, to a world where the sun has long since died out, and the remnants of humanity cluster in the Last Redoubt, a vast metal pyramid situated roughly where London used to be. Over the centuries a number of immense creatures have been approaching the pyramid, inch by inch, year by year. Now, held back by the Redoubt's defences, they wait for the time when they can move upon it and destroy it:

> The hugest monster of all, a living hill of watchfulness, the Watching Thing of the South. It brooded there, squat and tremendous, hunched over the pale radiance of the Glowing Dome ... a million years gone came it out of the blackness, and grew steadily nearer through twenty thousand years; but so slow that in no one year could a man perceive that it had moved.

The Night Land is a vision of immense imaginative power, which would be a classic of modern fantasy were it not for the style in which it is written. In order – one supposes – to establish the feeling of *antiquity* in this future vision, Hodgson adopted a mock-antiquated style which makes the book as near unreadable as it is possible to be. A later, abridged edition removed some of the worst excesses, but it remains a book best admired from afar.

Later writers, such as Clark Ashton Smith, also set stories in the far future, but until recently the most successful exponent of the form was Jack Vance, with his stories of the dying earth (most of which are included in two books: *The Dying Earth* and *The Eyes of the Overworld*). Here, our sun's life is drawing to its close:

> The east flushed the red of old blood, and presently the sun appeared, trembling like an old man with a chill. The ground was shrouded by mist; Cugel was barely able to see that they crossed a land of black mountains and dark chasms.

Under the red light of this ancient sun is an Earth populated by magicians and strange creatures – some evolved in the aeons which have passed since our time, some alien in origin. Magic works, though the spells are so difficult that even a practised magician can only memorise a few, and as soon as they are spoken they are forgotten. There is a sense of great antiquity: we meet, for instance, members of one cult who will not set foot on the ground, for by now all the soil of Earth is, or has been, the bones and flesh of men, and they do not wish to desecrate the great cemetery which the planet has become. Vance, too, adopts a formal and somewhat mannered style – though he does not approach the excesses of Hodgson – but the stories he tells in this setting tend to be sprightly picaresque adventures.

But it is Vance, if anyone, who is the precursor of the major work of fantasy set in the ancient future. This is Gene Wolfe's *The Book of the New Sun*, a novel some 1200 pages in length divided into four volumes – *The Shadow of the Torturer, The Claw of the Conciliator, The Sword of the Lictor* and *The Citadel of the Autarch*. Though published as self-contained novels they cannot really be read in any order than that of publication. There are no synopses of earlier volumes; the narrative is continuous; Wolfe's style is often

so cunning and oblique that anyone entering the novel in mid-stream will have no real idea what is going on. Indeed, the reader who starts at the beginning only discovers slowly and by carefully measured degrees what is *really* going on, though the adventures which are the story's surface are clear enough.

Wolfe has set himself the task of imagining his future world in as much detail as – for example – Tolkien's world, but without basing its customs, religion, flora and fauna, myths and beliefs on our own. Our world is lost well beyond the mists of antiquity for these people. We may occasionally perceive a hint of something familiar, but the interpretation put upon it in the novel is different and strange. Almost the only recognisable artifact in the whole sequence is a picture we encounter early in the first volume, which "showed an armoured figure standing in a desolate landscape. It had no weapon, but held a staff bearing a strange, stiff banner. The visor of this figure's helmet was entirely of gold, without eye slits or ventilation; in its polished surface the deathly desert could be seen in reflection..."

Although *we* may realise this to be an astronaut on the Moon, Severian, the narrator, does not. The Moon he knows is green and forested, and much closer to the Earth than in our day. In the million years or more that have passed since our day Earth has developed a space travelling civilisation, remnants of which remain; aliens have visited our world, and alien species have been introduced to replace vanished terrestrial ones; the sun is growing red and dim and, the stories have it, is collapsing in upon itself. Earth has become Urth. The central religion is built around the figure of the Conciliator, who will return as the New Sun, replacing the dying old sun and ushering in a new era of greatness.

The civilisation of this Urth is a curious mixture of feudalism and technology. It is ruled over by the shadowy figure of the Autarch, but his power becomes less secure as one moves

Preceding pages: The river Gyoll wound through Nessus like a great, weary snake. The city, immeasurably ancient, was a blend of every kind of architectural style.

away from his palace, the House Absolute. There is a fairly rigid caste system, of "exultants", "optimates" and "armigers" and so forth. The most elevated caste, the exultants, are hereditary and seem to have been so for so long as to form a partially distinct species, far taller (for instance) than other humans.

The main population centre is Nessus, a city so immense that it takes more than half of the first novel for the characters simply to cross it. Although countless people still live there, many of the houses now stand empty. Its architecture is immensely diverse: "As is the fashion in some parts of the city, most of these buildings have shops in their lower levels, though they had not been built for the shops but as guildhalls, basilicas, arenas, conservatories, treasuries, oratories, artellos, asylums, manufactuaries, conventicles, hospices, lazarets, mills, refectories, deadhouses, abattoirs and playhouses... Turrets and minarets bristled; lanterns, domes and rotundas soothed; flights of steps as steep as ladders ascended sheer walls; and balconies wrapped facades and sheltered them in the parterre privacies of citrons and pomegranates."

This extract gives a fairly typical idea of the novel's style, which is formal and elegant, studded with unfamiliar nouns some of which are revived archaisms and some of which are inventions. The effect is not intrusive; rather, it conveys with precision the vision of a world in which much that is familiar to the narrator cannot be made familiar to us. We cannot always be entirely sure what we are seeing, any more than a Stone Age man transported to the twentieth century could understand what he saw. This is a difficult tightrope to walk – too much strangeness and the reader loses interest – but Wolfe treads it with unfailing confidence. This is to a large extent because of the incidental inventiveness of so much of the book. For instance, people ride not only horses but also creatures called destriers. We are not sure what a destrier is, but a laconic note informs us that for military purposes they are fast enough to permit cavalry charges against high-energy armament! Again, one of the specifically alien creatures living on Urth is the alzabo, a predator which temporarily absorbs the mind of its prey, so that for a while after it has eaten a human it can speak with his voice.

The narrator of the novel is Severian, who begins the first volume as a young apprentice in the Guild of Torturers, whose task it is to carry out punishments ordained by Urth's legal systems, from torture - known in this world as "excruciation" - to execution. Throughout the novel Severian practises his profession and takes pride in his work. The subtle and often quite compelling arguments which Wolfe gives Severian to justify his actions and his function in his society are one of the cleverest means by which he establishes a world of different values from ours, yet one in which humans are clearly human. Severian

Below: *Each wall of Father Inire's octagonal room was a mirror. Overhead was a brilliant blue-white lamp, whose light was caught by the mirrors and reflected back and forth ad infinitum.*

records dispassionately his performance of acts which in another context would revolt us, but here he never loses our interest and identification.

No sooner has Severian been elevated from apprentice to journeyman of the guild than he betrays his position by conniving in the suicide of the Chatelaine Thecla, an imprisoned exultant with whom he has fallen in love. In punishment he is sent away from the guild's citadel, and from the city of Nessus, to become Lictor (i.e. torturer and executioner) of the city of Thrax. It is a long journey, fraught with dangers and full of adventures, though the bones of the story are quite simple. Severian journeys across Nessus, meeting on the way people whose paths will continue to intersect with his for the remainder of the novel. He accidentally comes into possession of a gem called the Claw of the Conciliator - a relic of strange power, seemingly able in certain circumstances to heal and even to revive the dead - and he resolves to return it to the

Pelerines, the religious group from whom it has been stolen. He becomes involved with the followers of Vodalus, an outlaw whose aim it is to overthrow the Autarch and restore mankind to its former glory. He visits the House Absolute, the Autarch's palace, where he meets the Autarch and discovers that, mysteriously, he too is one of the Vodalarii. Because Severian is setting down his story some time after the event we know that he is destined eventually to become Autarch himself.

As the story unfolds, so too does the scope and detail of Gene Wolfe's invented world. There are hints of strangeness at the beginning of *The Shadow of the Torturer*, but the early pages read very much like a traditional fantasy (though better-written than most) except for the revelation that the Matachin Tower, in which the torturers live, is actually the disused hulk of a spaceship. Even this, though, may be taken as a relic of an ancient and forgotten technology. Only as the novel progresses do we begin to appreciate the extent to which the magical future technology still infuses Urth; and only as Severian travels do we come to see the strangeness and grandeur of his world.

For the technology and its consequences one or two examples will give a flavour. In *The Claw of the Conciliator* Severian at first travels in the company of a man called Jason who, we gradually learn, has returned to Urth recently after a space voyage during which – because of a mishap and because of time-dilation effects associated with travel near the speed of light – many centuries, or even thousands of years, may have passed. We gradually realise that

Preceding pages: *The Botanical Gardens were enclosed in a building of glass. Curiously, each chamber seemed to grow larger the further one went into it. The Garden of Endless Sleep was the place where the avern, a deadly flower of alien origin, grew and bloomed. In its centre was a dark lake and a seemingly endless fen. The brown water acted as a preservative on corpses, which were weighted down with lead shot and sunk, their positions mapped so that they could be fished up, if desired.*

Opposite: *By the remote shore of Lake Diuturna was a high spur of rock, and at its summit a keep which seemed, at first sight, to be shaped like an enormous toadstool. The central column was a round stone tower, the lens-shaped metal structure floating above it a vast sky ship bringing a party of Hierodules to the castle of giant Baldanders.*

Jason has a metal hand, and then, a little later, that much of his body is metal too. We learn that he has been injured, and the damaged parts of his body have been replaced by the only spare parts available. We *then* learn that the spare parts were not the metal parts of his body, but those which are now flesh … Again, the most startling instances of advanced technology are the devices called mirrors, although Severian comments, "How foolish to call them mirrors. They are to mirrors as the enveloping firmament is to a child's balloon." They appear to be a kind of teleportation device, but how their silvered panels accomplish this is a matter of mystery. One set of these mirrors is found, startlingly, on the facing pages of a book in the House Absolute.

At first Nessus, for all its towers built of old spaceships and its varied architecture, is not overawing in its size. Not until we reach the city Wall, at the end of *The Shadow of the Torturer* do we truly grasp the scale on which Severian's ancestors have built. Most of the characters have lived so far from it that, as one puts it, "the wall was no more than a dark line on the northern horizon when we looked from the glass-roofed room at the top of our tower." As we near it we realise what an astonishing feat of building it is. Constructed of black metal, it is so high that, as Severian says, "There are few sorts of bird, I think, that would fly over it. The eagle and the great mountain teratornis, and possible the wild geese and their allies; but few others."

Even more impressive, perhaps, is the mountain to which Severian journeys in *The Sword of the Lictor*: a peak which has been carved into the likeness of a former Autarch, like Mount Rushmore multipled a thousand-fold. At its base is a deserted city, and it is guarded by gigantic metal statues, whose faces turn every day to follow the sun. Here Severian ascends to a room carved behind the eye of the statue, from which he is forced to make a perilous descent.

The Book of the New Sun is full of such wonders, but Wolfe does not present them in a manner designed to make the reader gawp; they are part and parcel of the future world which Severian, the narrator, accepts because it is *his* world.

The novel itself is long, complex, rich in detail and incident, but very subtle in its effects. Most epic fantasies are painted with a broad narrative brush and can be summarised simply: The Fellowship of the Ring must travel to Mordor and destroy the Ring in order to defeat Sauron; Thomas Covenant must defeat Lord Foul in order to preserve The Land. *The Book of the New Sun* is not so easy to precis, and one can predict that analysis of its levels of meaning will be a major occupation of sf critics for years to come. (A forthcoming Wolfe novel, independent of this one but sharing its setting, may make matters easier). Wolfe has established himself as one of the most oblique modern sf writers: an earlier book, *The Fifth Head of Cerberus*, for instance, presents a mystery to be solved: has a human being on another world been killed and his place taken by a shape-changing alien. We see an official sifting the clues, and we see his conclusion. We do not see how he reaches his conclusion: that is something we are expected to work out for ourselves by reading, as it were, over his shoulder. It is as if an Agatha Christie crime novel omitted the chapter in which Hercule Poirot explains the reasoning by which he unmasked the murderer.

Here, everything is filtered through Severian, who we know will become Autarch. He tells us time and time again that he has an eidetic memory; can recall every detail of his past life. He regards this as a curse. Yet there are inconsistencies in his account, in small details, which in another author might be put down to carelessness but in a writer as meticulous as Wolfe are clear evidence that Severian is not an infallible narrator he professes himself to be. To give just two examples: at the beginning of *The Claw of the Conciliator* he recalls the events of the first chapter of *The Shadow of the Torturer*, but there is a difference in the accounts. Again, in *The Sword of the Lictor* he refers to a pouch which has been made for him in order to keep the Claw of the Conciliator safe, and we are told on separate occasions that it is made of doeskin and, later, that it is of human skin. (The fact that Severian can calmly carry items made of human skin, like the pouch – perhaps – or the scabbard of his sword, is another of the differences which make him and his world strange to us.)

The story, then, is Severian's story, but it is not at first glance obvious precisely what that story *is*. There are, for instance, mysteries surrounding his origin (like all torturers he came into the guild as the child of a victim: but whose child was he?). These are the kind of subtleties that Wolfe works into his narrative, and which make it rewarding to reread in detail, if you so wish. But it is not necessary to do so: Wolfe is telling a long and complex story, not setting a cryptic examination. *The Book of the New Sun* **has** established itself, while its four volumes were still appearing, as one of the classics of modern fantasy, because of its unfailingly rich and elegant writing, and because of the immense detail and solidity of its far future world, Urth, which like Tolkien's Middle Earth, and like the other great realms of fantasy, seems to have been visited and written about, rather than being invented by the author.